# MARTÍN LÓPEZ

# MARTÍN LÓPEZ

## CONQUISTADOR CITIZEN OF MEXICO

by C. Harvey Gardiner

UNIVERSITY OF KENTUCKY PRESS

LEXINGTON MCMLVIII

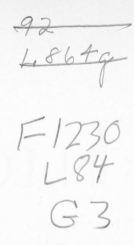

*The publication of this book has been possible partly by reason of a grant from
The Ford Foundation*

TO TEN-YEAR-OLD

# NELSON GARDINER

*who also wishes he had been there then*

# PREFACE

THIS is the story of a minor and reasonably representative man and his relationship to the significant period that saw the transfer of Spanish culture to the New World and the widening Hispanization of sixteenth-century American life.

Martín López is the man. Moving to America less than a quarter century after the Columbian discovery, he served as one of Cortés' initial followers throughout the conquest of Mexico—as infantryman, shipbuilder, and naval officer. After some additional campaigning in the field, he settled in infant Mexico City. Dabbling in commerce, agriculture, ranching, and mining, López almost ran the gamut of colonial economic interests. He also held two minor political posts. Socially he was husband successively to two Spanish women, father of ten children, godparent for numerous offspring of his friends, faithful friend to many, and implacable enemy of a few. Loyal and ever seeking yet another opportunity to serve his king, López also was faithful to himself, his hidalgo standards, and the conquistador class. A tough warrior and a tireless litigant, this transplanted Andalusian was a parent who worried about the educational opportunities and the job prospects of his sons and the dowries required by his marriageable daughters.

Sixteenth-century Spanish American life is usually presented through accounts of great leaders or significant institutions. With the former the greatness of one person—a conquistador, a churchman, or a viceroy—is so emphasized that the people led by him remain in hazy obscurity. On the other hand, the institutional presentation often describes full-blown political or judicial systems without any reference to the people for whom they were intended. Ignoring colonial society so completely—or generalizing about it so dangerously—many institutional studies depict Spanish legal theories rather than colonial reality.

The present work focuses attention on a minor figure in an effort to give perspective to the human factor operating within the framework of certain Spanish institutions and cultural patterns present in the sixteenth-century New World.

The status of Martín López is evident from the meager place allotted him in historical literature. Never once did Hernando Cortés name López in the course of five lengthy letters to his monarch. In similar fashion the eyewitness writers Andrés de Tapia, Bernardino Vázquez de Tapia, and the Anonymous Conqueror all consigned López to the considerable company of nameless men. Among the conquistador authors, Bernal Díaz del Castillo alone named the hidalgo shipwright from Seville. The garrulous infantryman identified Martín López and his contributions, but even this measure of attention, recorded in the last third of the sixteenth century, was not published until 1632. Meanwhile, one sixteenth-century writer, Francisco Cervantes de Salazar, lifted conquistador Martín López from utter anonymity. In the course of his second Latin dialogue, that humanist credited López with building the ships required for the capture of Tenochtitlán. A fuller statement of López' contributions to the events of 1520-1521, recorded by Cervantes de Salazar in his *Crónica,* remained unpublished until the twentieth century. However, by a noteworthy array of other sixteenth-century writers, including Martyr, Fernández de Oviedo, López de Gómara, Sahagún, Motolinía, Las Casas, Mendieta, Suárez de Peralta, and Alva Ixtlilxochitl, this minor figure was not mentioned.

First identified in a published work in 1554 by Cervantes de Salazar and next in Bernal Díaz' writing published eighty years later, Martín López has known no wide publicity during the last three centuries. While editing a pair of documents of the conquest, the late G. R. G. Conway in 1943 penned a provocative footnote about López. More recently, in 1948, the wave of writing on Cortés saw Guillermo Porras Muñoz and Manuel Romero de

Terreros produce skeletal views of certain aspects of López' career. Spanish and Mexican genealogical studies are unanimous in their failure to include his name. With the range of his activities pointing to him as an interesting figure, the sparsity of the record concerning him insists Martín López is indeed a minor one.

Assuming full responsibility for the facts and interpretations, the writer wishes to acknowledge assistance extended him by many persons. Lewis Hanke, Irving A. Leonard, and Alfred B. Thomas offered helpful criticism. Howard Cline, David C. Mearns, Stella Clemence, Schafer Williams, and John Finan of the staff of the Library of Congress and Ruth Lapham Butler of the Newberry Library, as well as Javier Malagón, France V. Scholes, and the late Arthur S. Aiton, helped me to materials. In Mexico, M. B. Trens, J. Ignacio Rubio Mañé, and Miguel Saldaña of the Archivo General de la Nación, a succession of directors and staff members of the Archivo de Notarías del Departamento del Distrito Federal, the staff of the Museo Nacional, Manuel Romero de Terreros, and Father José Bravo Ugarte were especially helpful. Two successive directors of the Archivo General de Indias assisted to the point of making unnecessary a trip to Spain. The staffs of the libraries of the University of Aberdeen and Cambridge University were similarly helpful.

The generosity of the John Simon Guggenheim Memorial Foundation has provided the final time period required to bring this study to completion. Added assistance came from Washington University.

From my son, who often pushed into my study and asked for still more of the story of Martín López, there came an unbelievable amount of challenge and inspiration. As he and I took swords down from the wall, squinted inquiringly at a map of Mexico, and relived moments of the sixteenth century, there must have been occasions when my wife, who always understood and often assisted, could have considered both of us crazy.

*Carbondale, Illinois*　　　　　　C. Harvey Gardiner
　*February 1, 1958*

# CONTENTS

# ILLUSTRATIONS

# CHAPTER I

# THE ANTECEDENTS OF ONE SPANIARD

ON HORSE and afoot over bleak plains and rugged mountains the crusading Christians had pushed ever southward across sun-baked, wind-swept Spain. Intermittently for centuries, Christian swords and lances had been at Moorish throats. Earlier and later than the Crusades, which took northerly knights off to the Holy Land, the cry from south of the Pyrenees had been: "The pagan Moor must go."

Led by Ferdinand III, most capable king and highly competent warrior, the Christian reconquest of Spain reached a climax. A spiritual urge drove the fighters on. From the drab-brown, rugged heights of the Sierra Morena, king and nobles and nobodies rode and marched down into the gardenlike valley of the Río Guadalquivir. There the silt-laden waters of the most navigable stream of the land meandered through a rich flat landscape

dedicated to grains and grapes, oranges and olives. Land to the
north had been rough, poor, uninviting, and unwanted, but this
in the south was smooth, rich, and desired. Many a footloose
fighter who had pushed on and on partly because he had seen so
little to stay him, now glimpsed a region he gladly would call
home.

In the midst of the valley, some fifty-odd miles from the Atlantic, lay Seville, the pearl of all Andalusia. For centuries when
they held it not, the Christians had coveted it from afar. Holding
it, they made Seville a focal point of Spanish life for the entire
peninsula. Its exposure to the lure of the wider world of the
Atlantic was later to convert it into headquarters for an empire.
Whether in medieval days, the dawn of discovery, or the high
noon of imperialism, to know Seville was to understand Spain.

The reconquest had unified Spanish energies in a supreme
undertaking that furthered the national state as well as the international church. Urged on by a religious zeal compounded of
humility and pride, the Spanish Christian had fought and bled
and, before dying, had served cross and crown. In the name of
meekness and kindness he girded himself in coat of mail, grasped
his Toledo blade, and boldly attacked an age-old enemy. Seek as
he might for honor and personal power—the prospect of hidalgo
status for the nobody, a dukedom for the count, a bishopric for
the priest, offices for many, and grants of land for all—his Spanish
way of life gravitated between the two poles of might and right,
of war and religion. Indeed, the city on the plain so closely
caressed on the left bank by the wide-sweeping waters of the
Guadalquivir was dominated in every section by the stone-upon-
stone reminders of fighting and faith.

Ten miles of surrounding wall, bolstered by scores of towers
but entered by a scant dozen gates, protected Seville's thousands
of residents. Fighters from Ferdinand's ranks received houses
strategically located throughout the community. Ever faithful in
the war of the reconquest, the great military orders like Santiago,
San Juan, Calatrava, and Alcántara had been richly rewarded
with properties which located their personnel at or close by key

positions on the periphery of the metropolis.[1] And as private Moslem wealth went to civilian warriors, so too minaret and mosque became campanile and church.

Sometimes the old was blended into the new; sometimes the old gave way to the new. The Alcazar, long the residence of Moorish rulers, became a royal palace for a succession of Spanish crowned heads. Some of its walls came down and new ones went up, but still the waters played from the Moorish fountains in the courtyards. Symbol of authority and might, the Alcazar was an anchor post in the south wall of the city whose defenses of stone and spirit and muscle had stayed the besieging forces of Ferdinand for fifteen months. When finally Seville had fallen, Ferdinand raised his Christian standard above the Alcazar. The small open area before it took the name Plaza del Triunfo. As speedily as churchmen could purify, the mosque turned cathedral and Ferdinand went northward across the plaza for prayer and thanksgiving.

In time the converted mosque was razed and the present cathedral was begun—to be finished a hundred and twenty years later. Visible from afar as it dominated the plain, the cathedral was the center of the region's religious life. With its high pillars, numerous aisles, and splendid iron screens, it possessed, despite its size, that peculiar warmth and intimacy the Spaniard knows in relation to his God. Great candles and clanging bells, scores of enormous hand-illuminated choir books, a gigantic font for the consecrated oil, and huge ironbound chests for charitable contributions—of such was compounded Spanish worship. With a rhythm deeply felt in the tempo of life, the cathedral drew traffic-stopping penitential processions during Holy Week; it was the seat of religious ceremonies in which councilman and countryman and count and cleric alike played their roles of ardent believers. Here royalty was entombed; here common folk commended themselves to God before sailing the wide waters to the Indies. Here, on the south side of the city, across the plaza from the seat of royal authority, stood the preeminent Spanish monument to God.

[1] Julio González (ed.), *Repartimiento de Sevilla* (2 vols., Madrid, 1951), opposite 358.

The twin forces of military might and religious devotion did not, however, monopolize the lives of Sevillians. Economically a crossroad for the rich region it dominated, Seville looked north to the sierras for timber, mineral products, and livestock. One of the city's most heavily used exits was the Córdoba gate, leading to the city of the same name three days' journey northward. Off to the west, across the river and behind the small community of Triana, lay the zone rich in olive and vine—land which, like the urban dwellings, had been allotted to Ferdinand's conquerors turned settlers. To the east and southeast stretched acres given over to orchards, orange groves, cereals, and other foodstuffs. From the south and the sea came fish and the commerce of the world. Up the Guadalquivir came ships and rumors, ships that dropped anchor just north of the point at which the waters of the Río Tagarete, slipping alongside the city wall, passed the Torre del Oro and joined the Guadalquivir. And scarcely were sails furled and hatches opened, before tales of distant lands were wafted across every plaza and up and down the narrow and sometimes crooked streets of Seville.

Men who had known the dignity of soldiering and men of social position—or aspiration thereto—abhorred the idea of working with their hands. So it was that converted Jews, ex-Moslems, Genoese, Frenchmen, and other moderately despised elements of the city produced much of the goods and performed many of the services that pumped a coursing life into the commerce of Seville. North and northeast from the cathedral area stretched the economic heart of the city, for there were situated the rows of shops maintained by weavers and tailors, dyers and embroiderers, leather-goods makers and producers of parchment. Proud of their labors with their hands, they were little people made great by virtue of quality of product and richness of tradition. Orderly and powerfully organized into guilds, these craftsmen brought dignity to the manual arts. From this district, alongside which on the south lay the Jewish quarter, moved the merchant caravans destined for Córdoba to the north and Algeciras, five days' journey toward the south.

Two decades before Columbus' memorable voyage the wharf area had been firmly established at the southern limit of the city, in the morning shadow of a pair of gates leading to the workaday heart of Seville. As physically secure as it was economically strategic, the district was but a stone's throw from the Torre del Oro and the local arsenal. There, opposite Triana and adjacent to the sandy stretch of shoreline so often employed for purpose of display, strange ships and stranger men discharged and loaded cargoes. With naked poles stretching skyward and loitering seamen heading for the attractions every great port city held for seafaring men, it was a time when the stay-at-home fell under the spell of the faraway. Long-silent seamen turned loquacious and spun yarns of recent adventures in distant climes. Many a son of Seville must have lost his heart to the sea. Especially here on the southwest side of the city, amid strong aromas and strange tongues, could one dream. Here it was easy to resolve someday to ride a ship down the Guadalquivir on the ebb tide.

Nor was everything not military and religious given over to work. Favored by productive soil, gentle warming breezes, and floods of sunshine, the Sevillians had reason to sing and dance, to express the rhythm pent up in fingers and toes and vocal chords. The cathedral was marked by the size of its organ and choir. Regularly and sedately the trained corps of boys danced before the high altar. Beyond the church, with guitar and castanet, with plaintive voice and stamping foot, music was even more sensuously a part of Spanish life. Outside her grilled window the Spanish lover, guitar in hand, serenaded his ladylove. Elsewhere the gypsies danced and sang the flamenco and vivacious spirits performed the seguidilla. In church, on the street, at the fair and the bullfight, at home—indeed, everywhere—one of the persistent throbs of Sevillian life was musical.

Fun-loving and frivolous, with little if any thought of the morrow, the citizens of Seville had compassion on those who had even neglected to give heed to the day. Lay religious brotherhoods, often the charitable extensions of the professional trade guilds, underwrote the operation of numerous humanitarian

services intended to ease the way of the orphan, the aged, the
sick, the destitute, and even the indolent. So commonly did
generous instincts well up in man and cause him to share his
worldly goods with him who approached with outstretched hand
and prayer on lips, that Seville bred a widening corps of profes-
sionals who looked upon begging as their careers. The dignity
of begging and the concomitant indignity of labor were furthered
by overly generous monks and nuns whose monasteries and convents became daily dispensaries of food.

This was the city for which affection had led the Spaniard to
say, "To whom God loves He gives a house in Seville." This
was the city in which, a few years before the springtime of 1492
brought final Christian victory to crusading Ferdinand and Isabel,
life began for one Martín López.

Martín López' family, one of the oldest Spanish households of
the city, lived on Calle Caldereros, on the northwest side of
Seville.[2] South of the San Juan gate, the street dead-ended into
the city wall and the Guadalquivir River on the west. A few
blocks north of Calle Caldereros stood the headquarters of the

[2] Because of variations in available evidence, the date of Martín López' birth
is vague. See Información de los méritos y servicios de Martín de la Mezquita
(1540, 1559, 1573, 1598), in Francisco del Paso y Troncoso Collection (Museo
Nacional, Mexico City), Leg. 95; G. R. G. Conway (ed.), La Noche Triste: Documentos: Segura de la Frontera en Nueva España, año de MDXX (Mexico City,
1943), 86; Mexico, Doc. XXXI, fol. 15, in Harkness Collection (Library of Congress); "Información recibida en México y Puebla el año de 1565, a solicitud
del gobernador y cabildo de naturales de Tlaxcala, sobre los servicios que prestaron
los tlaxcaltecas a Hernán Cortés en la conquista de México, siendo los testigos
algunos de los mismos conquistadores," Biblioteca Histórica de la Iberia, XX
(1875), 113; Martín López, Conquistador—Documents, 1528-1574, pp. 149, 157,
161, 165, 170, 174, 178, 182, in Conway Collection (University of Aberdeen).
The consensus places López' birth in the interval between 1487 and 1490.

Discussion of Martín López' ancestry, unless otherwise indicated, is based upon
two sources: Luis Vilar y Pascual, Diccionario histórico genealógico y heráldico
de las familias ilustres de la monarquía española (8 vols., Madrid, 1859-1866),
VII, 381-91; and a mass of Spanish court proceedings of the 1530's which, when
incorporated into certain family records of the early seventeenth century, became
known as the Nobiliario de Martín López Ossorio, in Conway Collection (Library
of Congress). The genealogical data within those family records derives from
court testimony presented by eleven witnesses: see Miscellaneous Documents
Relating to Martín López and Other Papers, 3-32, in Conway Collection (Cambridge University).

military order of San Juan. There, too, on the north stood
the stone and tile rectangular tower of Fadrique, built just a
handful of years after Martín López' warrior ancestor had entered
the city with King Ferdinand in 1248. An even shorter distance
to the south towered San Vicente, a onetime mosque dating
from the fourteenth century, which long since had attained respectability as a parish church. San Vicente was the church of
infant Martín's parents, Cristóbal Díaz Narices and Estefanía
Rodríguez. Flanked on north and south by two of the mightiest
forces in Spanish history, Martín López of Calle Caldereros was
destined to blend the ways of the strong right arm and the com-
passionate heart when later he took passage down the nearby
Guadalquivir for the distant Indies.

Not long before the arrival of this youngster, the Inquisition
had come to Seville. Such, however, would not ruffle the ways
of young Martín, child that he was of at least nine clearly
identifiable generations of orthodox Christians. The property on
Calle Caldereros as well as the vineyards, olive groves, and fig
orchards, imposing and income-producing properties, had been
a grant from Ferdinand III. Year after year in the 1480's, as
Seville contributed hundreds of horsemen and thousands of foot
soldiers for the final fighting in Granada, this family that had
helped to win the city of Seville continued to serve in the battles
that ended Moslem power in Spain. Pride, training, religion,
tradition—all compelled such service.

At a moment when Martín López still was too young for
school, Spaniards began to plan voyages to the ends of the earth.
In March of 1493, the tall, weatherbeaten Genoese whose nautical
plans had stamped him a dreamy-eyed fool in the minds of countless skeptics was back in the port from which he had sailed seven
months earlier. Having discovered a new world, Columbus had
returned to tiny Palos. Preceded by good reports and even better
rumor, he hastily made his way toward Barcelona, the temporary
seat of Spain's peripatetic royalty.

It was the matchless brilliance of springtime in Seville that

Palm Sunday when the Great Discoverer passed that way on his northbound journey of triumph, everywhere hailed for his nautical success. "As he passed through the busy, populous city of Seville, every window, balcony, and housetop, which could afford a glimpse of him, is described to have been crowded with spectators."[3]

Exhilaration produced curiosity and interest. The city, long a southern terminus for Spanish life, swiftly became the springboard of imperial activity. Not only did her own adventure-minded men of all ages contract the "Indies fever," her peculiarly strategic position soon dictated that she also play the role of seaward funnel for the emigrants of central and northern Spain.

In the next decade, that saw three more voyages by Columbus as well as expeditions by other men, Ferdinand and Isabel centralized their New World endeavors. Fortunately placed and even more fortunately the object of royal favor, Seville became the official headquarters of New World enterprise. There expeditions formed and sailed away; there too they returned. By 1503, when Martín López was in his teens, the Casa de Contratación had been established in his home town. There officers of the crown acquired supplies, provisioned ships, licensed pilots, screened emigrants—everything necessary for the success of the first overseas European empire. There, one day in 1504, a nineteen-year-old youth from Medellín named Hernando Cortés took ship for the island of Española. The vessels that moved the men and materials to the Indies dropped anchor around the first bend in the river to the south, and young Martín López of Calle Caldereros did not grow to maturity in Seville without being aware of them. In fact, family affairs possibly inclined him all the more readily to a keen interest in the opportunities beyond the horizon.

As he approached maturity, young López did not need much wisdom to realize his prospects were doubly limited. The gentlemanly career at arms, high road to enrichment and ennoblement,

---

[3] William H. Prescott, *History of the Reign of Ferdinand and Isabella* (2 vols., New York, 1884), I, 366.

had suffered eclipse in Spain. His ancestor who had entered Seville with Ferdinand III had been rewarded for his services with twenty *aranzadas*[4] of olive and fig trees, six aranzadas of vineyard, two aranzadas for gardening purposes, and six plots of land—with as many yoke of oxen—for general agriculture—as well as the house on Calle Caldereros.[5] But that had been in a day with pagans to be defeated and lands to be added to the royal domain. Now in Spain there were no Moors to dispossess, no regions to be won, no properties to be divided.

When Martín's illustrious ancestor Alvar Pérez Ossorio served King Henry well by defending Venavente, Henry had named him a count. In time, later counts of Villalobos became marquises of Astorga as well, and the powerful line of Martín's forebears garnered even more wealth, greater power, and additional prestige —all for services rendered to the crown. But this century that was just beginning had ended such opportunities.

Martín quite probably was not the first-born son of a man who was himself a third son. The dismal prospect faced by his father, Cristóbal Díaz Narices, is evident in his very name. Unlike his pair of older brothers, Martín's father did not bear the name Ossorio. Without prospects from the powerful family, Martín's father had been named for his mother's family. In fact, those grandparents of young Martín were also in a disadvantageous position, for grandfather Martín Álvarez Ossorio was likewise a third son. As a son of the third son of a third son, Martín soon knew the easy way of automatic inheritance was not to be his lot. On the proud but poor margin of a great family, Martín López was a young man in need of a career.

Above the door of the house he knew so well on Calle Caldereros was emblazoned the family's coat of arms: two red wolves prancing on a golden field, above which was a helmet surmounted by a

---

[4] For this and subsequent foreign-language terms for which the meaning is not given in the text, see the glossary, pp. 187-88.

[5] Each of the two hundred hidalgo founders of Seville received this minimum grant; see Diego Ortiz de Zúñiga, *Annales eclesiásticos, y seculares de la muy noble, y muy leal ciudad de Sevilla* (Madrid, 1677), 66-71.

crown. Above and around it all was the legend, "These live as
they die, and die doing their duty."[6] A proudly eloquent motto
for a family which had fought the battles of Christian reconquest
and royal consolidation for centuries, it stood, at the dawn of the
sixteenth century, a taunt to one who could not clearly see his
duty close at home.

Martín López naturally breathed a spirit of adventure. That,
at least, the Ossorios and the Spain in which they had thrived had
bequeathed him. Fortunately his home city of Seville opened the
door to the kind of career his motherland otherwise denied him.

By 1508 the Casa de Contratación had enlarged its original
personnel, not least among whom was the new pilot major, Amer-
igo Vespucci, who was accidentally to lend his name to all the
Western Hemisphere. The number of vessels bound for the Indies
increased enormously. The Spaniards were improving charts and
tightening pilot regulations. Meanwhile, thousands of Spaniards
had followed Columbus. His own subsequent voyages had resulted in the first colony, Española, and the first municipality,
Santo Domingo. There the Spanish emigrant expressed in precise
formula his love of urban ease. True, some had gone armed with
agricultural tools, but that which they had disdained in Spain did
not prove captivating in the New World. In the New as well as
the Old World the Spaniard continued to scorn manual labor.

Even before Christopher Columbus' inadequacies as an administrator had led to his displacement by royal authority, age-old
Spanish patterns born of the period of the reconquest at home
were at work in the Indies. Men who fought the Indians were
rewarded. New-won lands were assigned the conquistadors. And
as defeated natives found it impossible to pay annual tributes in
precious metal, they gradually came to work for the white over-
lord. Employing this labor force in farming or ranching or
mining, the conquistador who might have been a nobody could
become a person of consequence on Española.

Within a decade after its initial discovery the New World had

6 *Estos viven que murieron muriendo como deuieron.*

become a goal for thousands. Fray Nicolás de Ovando, setting out
for the governorship of Española in 1502, was accompanied by a
fleet of more than thirty ships loaded with settlers. In fewer than
a dozen years thereafter, seventeen towns were established on
Española alone. Meanwhile, even as the second decade of the
sixteenth century got under way, the manpower of Española and
the officials in its capital, Santo Domingo, launched activities that
made that island the hub of a widening Caribbean empire. Almost
simultaneously San Juan, Puerto Rico, was established, Jamaica
overrun, and Cuba conquered. Cuba, destined in turn to play
springboard for the invasion of the Mexican mainland, was sub-
dued by a conquistador throng headed by Diego Velázquez. At
his side were men like Pánfilo de Narváez, his most competent
field commander, Hernando Cortés, an administrative assistant
who was to know his own bright day of leadership, and the
Dominican friar Bartolomé de las Casas, a Sevillian by birth and
a humanitarian by inclination who painted Spanish-Indian relations in somber word pictures. By 1515 seven Spanish settlements
dotted the Cuban landscape.

Everywhere it was the same story. Vigorous, adventure-minded
men of limited means and limitless energies sought to widen the
royal domain, improve their own economic and social lot, and
advance the cause of God as they promised to carry out the
regulations inspired by the pious Isabel.

Seville's essentially agrarian base of her economic life was
modified by the rising tempo of imperial commerce in all kinds of
products. Nor did the nobility and other well-born Sevillians
disdain the moneymaking opportunities their city offered. In
this period was born the truth of Alarcón's statement:[7]

> Es segunda maravilla
> Un caballero en Sevilla
> Sin rama de mercader.

[7] Quoted in Antonio Dominguez Ortiz, *Orto y ocaso de Sevilla: estudio sobre
la prosperidad y decadencia de la ciudad durante los siglos xvi y xvii* (Seville,
1946), 52.

In the quarter century after 1492, years that brought Martín
López to maturity in Seville, scores upon scores of ships had sailed
thence, carrying thousands to the Indies. With a minimum of
paperwork and six to eight gold ducats for passage and food, one
could sail direct to San Juan in Puerto Rico, Santo Domingo in
Española (which had the heaviest traffic), or Santiago in Cuba.[8]

By 1516—by then he was between twenty-five and thirty years
old—Martín López made the decision that cast his lot with the
New World. Long enough aware of the lures of the Indies so
thick upon the tongues of Sevillians, of all Spaniards, he elected
a career beyond the Atlantic. Heir of all the physical and moral
drives that had spurred Spaniards onward for generations, he
knew youth in changing Seville, in a shifting climate of opinion
which prepared him admirably for the measure of adaptability
the New World would demand of him.

On September 26, 1516, Martín López entered his name upon
the register of the Casa de Contratación as one intending to
migrate to the Indies.[9] The following week Bartolomé Sánchez,
master of the *Santa María de Luz,* was busy loading merchandise
of biscuit-maker Luis Fernández aboard his vessel preparatory to
setting sail for Santiago, Cuba, seat of Governor Velázquez'
authority in that recently won island. Was Martín López a
passenger aboard the *Santa María de Luz?* If not, he had additional sailing opportunities in the weeks ahead.[10] For him, as for
most other Spanish emigrants, the date of departure, ship, shipmaster, cost of passage, landing place, and date of landing are all
unknown. Precisely what he had done in Spain we do not know;
what he would do in the New World he did not know. Like
many other Spanish emigrants, Martín López went to America to
emerge from anonymity. Nor did this son of Seville go empty-

---

[8] José María Ots Capdequí, *Catálogo de los fondos americanos del Archivo de
Protocolos de Sevilla* (3 vols., Madrid, 1930-1932), I, 270-344 *passim;* II, 39-40;
III, 37, 47.

[9] Cristóbal Bermúdez Plata, *Catálogo de pasajeros a Indias durante los siglos
XVI, XVII y XVIII* (3 vols., Seville, 1940), I, 156.

[10] Ots Capdequí, I, 317-21.

handed. With him went a sizable supply of wine, clothing, food-stuffs, and merchandise.[11] López could hardly have required all these things in such quantities. Was the Indies-bound Sevillian of hidalgo status, aware of trans-Atlantic needs and prices, about to embark on a commercial career?

[11] López, 1528-1574, p. 60, Conway Coll. (Aberdeen); Martín López, Conquistador—Documents, 1529-1550, p. 121, Conway Collection (Library of Congress).

# CHAPTER II

# A CONQUISTADOR PUTS ASIDE
# HIS SWORD

**W**ELL-ENDUED physically, Martín López was a tall, strong man of enormous energy —tall enough to make a singular contribution at one crucial moment of the conquest, strong enough to march countless kilometers and to recover from multiple wounds, four of them suffered on a single occasion. He weathered physical privation and withstood the shock of heavy financial loss. Triumphing over numerous and varied hardships as he lived eight and a half decades, López was an uncommon man, even among the peculiarly hardy breed of sixteenth-century Spaniards found on New World frontiers.

López, too, was a man of remarkable physical courage. He possessed that kind commonly related to group action and in addition knew another brand of courage, for he often pioneered. Fearless and never acknowledging defeat, López fought endlessly, with weapons and with words, being both a man of action and ideas.

When Bernal Díaz del Castillo termed Martín López "a good soldier," the chronicler garnished, with modest understatement, the braggadoccio which abounds in his writing. López lent funds to his commander in support of the common cause, he brought along personal servants who were capable artisans as well as brave fighters, he provided supplies which relieved the needs of numerous colleagues. Unprotestingly he accepted the most routine of duties. He was also the warrior who engineered a new weapon for Cortés' most trying military moment.

In days of conquest, and long years thereafter, López was a commonly encountered paradox, a man who possessed the common denominators of all Spanish manhood and yet exhibited unimpeachable individuality. Initially an infantryman, then successively a shipbuilder, naval officer, and cavalryman, López was equally able to give and take orders. An even-tempered man who did not boast of the number of battles he had fought nor of the Indians he had slain, he entered the conquest with ideals tempered by the reality of sound judgment. Loyal to commander and king, López knew additional loyalties to his conquistador class and to himself, loyalties which often led to frictions and frustrations.

Basically civilian by nature—he shouldered arms only once after 1525 and then under conditions that suggest his was not a free choice—López' personality was persistently paradoxical in the long half century of his settled life. The years that found him husband, parent, neighbor, rancher, officeholder, petitioner, and litigant underscored the traits of the man.

Religiously pious, López married in the church, had his children baptized, served as godfather for numerous offspring of his friends, gave sons to the clergy, and treated his Indians in a manner evoking no criticism. In so doing, he was both at peace and at war with patterns of conquistador behavior.

Economically acquisitive, he knew no days of real toil after the close of his fighting career. Loot and land were supplemented by posts and petitions that aimed at salaries and other income-producing opportunities. Rural rancher, urban landlord, and dabbler in commercial speculations, López possessed the means which elevated him above many and yet so left him beneath the top that he dedicated much of his remarkable persistence to bettering his economic status.

Socially gregarious and generous, he was loving husband, doting parent, generous neighbor, hospitable conquistador. Proud of his Spanish blood, he successively married Spanish women of acceptable social position. Carefully his children sought Spanish husbands and wives. Democratic to the extent that he demanded opportunities to rise, López also safeguarded the concept of social stratification.

Intellectually he was ever a man at war with himself—simultaneously the realist and the idealist, the conserver and the changer, the age-old Spaniard and the emergent American. Imaginative and conforming, consistent and inconsistent, generous and greedy, cultured and crude, aggressive and passive, rapacious and considerate, exaggerating and truthful, indolent and ambitious, cooperative and contentious, simple and complex—of such was the contradictory nature of Martín López.

That chapter in Martín López' life between his arrival, most probably in Santo Domingo—though possibly in Cuba—in the weeks ending 1516 or beginning 1517, and his enlistment in the ranks of Cortés' force sometime in late 1518 is closed to us. On the basis of his apparent station and financial condition at the time of the conquest of Mexico, however, one suspects these were months wherein the young Spaniard, possessing a fairly ample purse, moved about in search of an undertaking in which he could profitably invest both his physical energies and his money. We do not know how long he had been in Cuba before he encountered Cortés, but once he affiliated himself with the magnetic man from Medellín, he dedicated his purse as well as his person to his undertaking.

Meanwhile, Spaniards in Cuba were growing restless. What had happened on the neighboring island of Española in earlier years was repeating itself in Cuba during the 1510's. As Columbus for his discoveries had been made governor of Española, so Diego Velázquez, leader of the conquest of Cuba, had come to head that colony. As ship after ship had disgorged human cargo upon the shores of Española, so now they landed men on Cuba. As many of those early birds on Española had risen to local prominence, so it happened on Cuba. From Baracoa and Santiago on the east to Sancti Spiritus, Trinidad, and Habana to the west, Spanish-planted towns sprang into existence. Barely breaking the sweep of palm trees, the small towns nestled near the sandy Caribbean shores— flimsy, thatched shelters close upon the plaza, within a stone's throw of church and seat of local administration. As on Española, the Spaniards in Cuba sought lives of ease—tributes paid in shining metal by the Indians, offices and land granted by the crown. And, as in Española, the supply in Cuba had been insufficient to quench the Spanish thirst for gold. Some men settled down and married, or sent back home for their wives. Others, footloose, became restless. And even the settled citizens complained that the Indians who could not bring them gold took to the hills and the swamps to escape service under their new overlords. Before he could bring himself to onerous toil, the Spaniard would rather search elsewhere for natives whose labor might give him the ease he sought.

In early 1517 one Cuban rancher, Francisco Hernández de Córdoba, headed a labor-procurement expedition of three vessels and slightly more than a hundred men. From this armed reconnaissance, rumors of richer lands quickly displaced the idea of replenishing the supply of workers in Cuba, and a second expedition, led by a kinsman of Governor Velázquez, set out in the spring of 1518. Juan de Grijalva repeated his predecessor's probing of the giant peninsula of Yucatan and then pushed farther on, northward along the Gulf coast of modern Mexico, before returning to Cuba and a governor who dreamed ambitiously of administering a wider, richer jurisdiction.

These two minor undertakings—Grijalva had commanded only four ships and approximately two hundred men—knew common experiences: intense opposition from the natives, proof of denser and wealthier Indian cultures than had been found elsewhere in the Indies, and a consuming passion among the survivors to return once more to the shore of that newest land of opportunity. In all this, Cuba was still following essentially the Española pattern, because these probing reconnaissances, so like certain voyages from Española to Cuba and Puerto Rico and Jamaica somewhat earlier, pointed to a further fanning out of Spanish imperial enterprise.

With Hernández de Córdoba dead and Grijalva adjudged less than forceful enough to meet the situation, Governor Velázquez turned to a trusted aide from the Española and Cuban campaigns, Hernando Cortés, then 33 years old. With official backing, which included Velázquez' promise of some ships for the forthcoming third and considerably larger venture, Cortés proclaimed the nature of his expedition and invited adventure-minded men to join him. No one town or single section of Cuba could afford him all the ships he desired, the men he needed, the supplies he required. In the autumn and winter of 1518-1519 Cortés went up and down the island enrolling approximately five hundred men for the expedition he was about to lead westward. A few men of wealth had capital to invest in the expedition. A more numerous group brought to the undertaking nothing more than enthusiasm and strong right arms. Some were debtors. Between the extremes of wealth and poverty were some men who not only took care of their own needs but also, on occasion, provided for the wants of some of their less fortunate colleagues and made small contributions toward financing the total force.

Whereas the men like Cristóbal de Olid, Pedro de Alvarado, and a half-score more who brought reputations, experience, and means to the undertaking quickly became captains on horseback, the lesser men were likewise important. Such a one was blacksmith Hernán Martín.

Plagued as he was by unseaworthy vessels—evidently no ships

had been built in Cuba despite the royal permission of late 1516 —Cortés needed men like Hernán Martín. Before some of the least seaworthy craft could join the growing armada rendezvousing at the western tip of the island, Cortés ordered Hernán Martín, at San Cristóbal de la Habana, to produce nails and bolts, pins and spikes for their repair. When finally the men embarked for the mainland of America, blacksmith Martín carried his forge and other tools aboard the *Guecho*.[1] Carpenters, as well as other blacksmiths, joined the Cortés expedition, for the workers in wood included such recruits as the brothers Pedro and Miguel de Mafla, Juan Martínez Narices, Andrés Núñez, Diego Hernández, and Sebastián Rodríguez among others.[2] Although lacking the glamour of armor and arquebus and cannon, the hammers and saws of these artisans were destined to play indispensable roles in the months ahead.

Among those enrolling in the cause of Cortés was Sevillian-bred Martín López, who was neither a man of great wealth and prestige nor a penniless artisan.

Martín López bore signs of his hidalgo origin as he enlisted under the banner of Cortés. His bearing and dress marked him a person of quality, a man of position, a Spaniard of standing. Furthermore, he had at hand all the equipment needed for sea voyage and land campaign—and a full measure of that Spanish common denominator of the day, high hopes. Compared with most of the men of the rapidly forming expedition, Martín was well off.

Attesting his personality and wealth was the contribution he made to the expedition. In addition to equipping himself, López possessed a surplus of some things. An enormous quantity of wine, two or three boxes of clothing beyond his own needs, a miscellaneous array of unspecified merchandise, and a variety of foodstuffs, among which bread and vinegar can be identified, were

[1] Información de los méritos y servicios de Hernán Martín (1531), Paso y Troncoso Coll., Leg. 95.
[2] C. Harvey Gardiner, *Naval Power in the Conquest of Mexico* (Austin, 1956), 64-65.

included among the commodities he took aboard ship in Cuba. One wonders if López intended to engage in trade with the natives.

Such a vague statement of his property, referring as it does only to things adapted to use during the conquest, renders impossible any real assessment of his financial status in 1518. The two pipes of wine—possibly approximating 1,000 liters—the only definitely stated quantity of any of the items mentioned, did represent considerable value. In the mid-1520's, under Spanish authority which already had established maximum prices for the liquid product of the vine in infant Mexico City, wine varied between 65 and 120 pesos per pipe.[3] The fact that three personal servants accompanied him does give some idea of his status, however.

A charitable nature, coupled with such a stockpile, repeatedly found López playing host to some of his poorer shipmates between Cuba and the final landing place on the coast of the continent. He invited two, three, or even four men at a time to dine with him. The daily regularity with which a number of his comrades in arms sat at his table constituted no inconsiderable contribution toward the provisioning of the group with whom he spent weeks aboard ship.

Two of the menservants accompanying López were brothers, Miguel and Pedro de Mafla, both of whom, carpenters by trade, were to aid him greatly in subsequent shipbuilding enterprises. A third person particularly close to the man from Seville was Juan Martínez Narices, a cousin who, dying in battle, never tasted the fruits of final victory.

No data are available regarding the name of the vessel on which López crossed from Cuba to New Spain. Among his shipmates, however, were Juan Gómez de Herrera and Andrés de Trujillo, both of whom affirm the well-being and charitable nature of

---

[3] *Actas de cabildo de la ciudad de México,* ed. by Ignacio Bejarano and others (26 vols., Mexico City, 1889-1904), I, 107. For representative listings of wine prices by the pipe between February, 1527, and November, 1528, see A. Millares Carlo and J. I. Mantecón, *Indice y extractos de los protocolos del Archivo de Notarías de México, D. F.* (2 vols., Mexico City, 1945-1946), I, nos. 350, 600, 857, 876, 1675.

López at this early stage of his New World career, although some extravagance possibly attended the words of fellow conquistador Gerónimo Ruiz de la Mota when he remarked, "Among the conquistadors he [Martín López] was the one who brought most and was fitted out best to travel in foreign parts."[4]

Martín López also put some cash at the disposal of Cortés for the outfitting of the expeditionary force, money which had come to hand as he marketed his wares in the Antilles. Lázaro Guerrero, destined to enter New Spain with Narváez in 1520, witnessed the loan of 325 pesos, even helping to weigh the gold. "No one in this world has a better man in his service than I have. Look what Martín López has loaned me to meet our present needs," Cortés is reported to have said at that moment.[5]

Two eyewitnesses of this episode state that López also offered Cortés additional funds. Precise dates are not known for either the 325-peso loan or the offer of additional monetary aid, but the loan probably took place while the expedition was forming in Cuba.

Between mid-February and the Easter season of 1519, the eleven-ship expedition that had rendezvoused at Cape San Antonio crossed to the mainland, widening its knowledge and whetting its curiosity by means of frequent contacts with the natives along the shores of Yucatan and Tabasco. A castaway Spaniard who knew the Maya tongue and a Mexican maiden who knew both the Maya and Nahuatl languages enriched Cortés' supply of information. Finally the anchors dropped for the last time, almost in the shadow of the island of San Juan de Ulúa, and the company streamed ashore to resume the ways of landsmen.

Horses and weapons, the cassava bread and live pigs, carpenters' tools and the blacksmiths' forges, all went ashore along with the unconsumed supplies of Martín López.

---

[4] López, 1528-1574, pp. 57, 60, 66, 69-70, 75, 78, 84, 88, 93, 104, 109, 112-13, 117, 124, 126, 130, 133, 137-38, 140, Conway Coll. (Aberdeen); López, 1529-1550, pp. 119, 126, 135, 137, 141-42, 149, 156, 162, Conway Coll. (LC).

[5] López, 1528-1574, p. 69, Conway Coll. (Aberdeen).

In that area, as Cortés picked up details of the wealth and high civilization of the Indians of the interior, he learned that native dissensions existed which might aid the Spaniards, and he saw the need for a base of operations. Here he established a municipality bearing the revealing name of Villa Rica de la Vera Cruz. Surrendering to this town government the authority conceded him by Velázquez, Cortés speedily had himself renamed captain general to free himself from Cuban authority. History was still repeating itself, for Velázquez also had rebelled from the Española authority which had commissioned him.

Cortés' plans to move into the interior faced opposition. The seamen did not want to leave their ships and the sea; the pro-Velázquez men refused to accept the widening ambitions of their stockily built, bearded commander. In a bold move for unity and support, Cortés destroyed all his ships save one. On that last surviving vessel, once it had been strengthened by metallic fittings hammered out by blacksmith Hernán Martín and his compatriots of hammer and forge,[6] Cortés sent two of his captains, Francisco de Montejo and Alonso Hernández Puertocarrero, to the Spanish court as his spokesmen. With the naming of a garrison force for Vera Cruz and the formulation of an alliance with the Totonac Indians, Cortés was ready, by late summer of 1519, to push into the hinterland.

In September, in the province of Tlaxcala, the Spaniards met the most vigorous opposition they had ever known in the New World, and in so doing, won the most loyal allies they could have hoped for in the developing conquest of Mexico. From proud, independent Tlaxcala the invaders, reinforced by thousands of its Mexican-hating natives, moved on to populous Cholula, religious capital of the Aztec realm. There, thanks to the alertness and loyalty of Marina, the Indian interpreter, a bloody ambush which might have made corpses of all the Spaniards was averted. While the Spaniards pushed westward from Cholula, the Mexican emperor Montezuma was paralyzed by indecision. Men whom he

6 Información de Hernán Martín (1531), Paso y Troncoso Coll., Leg. 95.

already thought possessed godly attributes now repeatedly demonstrated their superhuman qualities, winning victory after victory, averting his best laid strategems and luring more and more discontented natives to the side of the invading host. What could he do now but invite them into his capital Tenochtitlán?

Midautumn found the mixed Spanish-Tlaxcalan force poised, ready to spill into the heartland of his empire, the Valley of Mexico. Via the trail that led between the snowcapped peaks of Ixtaccihuatl and Popocatepetl, the ambition-driven handful of white men moved, with their Tlaxcalan bearers and warriors, into the lake-studded valley so generously dotted with communities. Accompanied by a select group of his nobles, Montezuma went to the edge of his island capital to greet the strangers marching over the southern causeway across the waters of Lake Texcoco. Invited to take up residence as royal guests in a palace within the city, the invaders moved into the heart of the greatest native metropolis of the New World, Tenochtitlán, a city of 300,000 inhabitants.

Tenochtitlán was at once center and symbol of Aztec culture. Founded in 1325 on islands in Lake Texcoco as a refuge from their more numerous and powerful neighbors in the Valley of Mexico, Tenochtitlán's growth reflected expanding Aztec power. Initially a place of retreat, it became the springboard for the increasingly complex pattern of Aztec imperialism. The rulers lived in spacious palaces in the heart of the community, close upon the central plaza and towering pyramid dedicated to religious rites. Religion and politics were closely entwined, with Montezuma a twin-natured leader of church-state affairs unlike any of his European counterparts. Polytheism gave rise to a numerous and powerful priesthood, with practices smacking of faith and superstition, some of which, like the legend of Quetzalcoatl—the fair god who had departed the land with a promise he would return—the Spaniards exploited to promote inertia and disunity among the natives. A sizable military caste buttressed Aztec religious and political unity. Growing power and prestige had rapidly widened the empire in the century preceding the arrival of the Spaniards. Compounding the Aztec confederation by military victory and diplomatic alliance, Aztec authority radiated from the island base of Tenochtitlán, established itself among the lakefront communities beyond the three rubble-filled causeways which connected the city with the mainland, and reached out to subjugate the hinterland—the mountain-rimmed, oval-shaped 2,000-square-mile highland Valley of Mexico. With its millions of inhabitants, the valley became the widened core of Aztec might. Then ambitious merchants and ready warriors spilled over the valley's rugged walls. With varying success they moved in every direction, conquering and consolidating, for in the wake of the warrior moved the tribute collector. In time Aztec power ranged from Gulf to Pacific, with more than one peripheral portion recently acquired and ill digested when Cortés and his followers appeared on the scene.

Hub of empire for an Indian world, majestic Tenochtitlán, like a magnet, had drawn the Spaniards under Cortés to it. Once there, the strangers marveled at it and its people. Industrious and disciplined, the natives spent their lives in devotion to family and state and religion. The quality of their cloth, the proportions of their buildings, the nature of their weapons, the range of their agricultural products, their organized markets, their obedience to god and emperor—all marked theirs as the most advanced native way of life the Spaniards had encountered in the New World. Lovers of flowers and blood, advocates of filial affection and human sacrifice, submissive and aggressive, the paradoxical Indian nature might have led introspective Spaniards to think of their own people. Some wore richly embroidered robes and walked in dignity; others, ill-clad, stumbled along under oppressive loads that stamped them beasts of burden. A city and a culture of strengths and weaknesses, of things to be coveted and to be abhorred, Tenochtitlán and the Aztec way of life intrigued the Spanish guests.

During the second week of November the Spaniards who had

lightheartedly entered the city with confidence born of unbroken victories came to feel increasingly ill at ease. For land warriors the lake setting, the causeways, and the island metropolis produced a sense of growing insecurity. Unlike anything previously encountered, the geography of the heart of the Valley of Mexico served to sober the invaders to the realization that their position in canal-laced Tenochtitlán was an unsafe one, several miles from a mainland which they could reach only by means of narrow causeways of stone and rubble pierced by numerous watercourses spanned by removable bridges. Captain general and common soldier alike wished to remedy the situation. One of two things had to be done: either the invaders must withdraw from the city, or they had to improve their military position on the island. The idea of retreat received no serious consideration; it just did not comport with Spanish military experience in the New World, especially with the brilliant series of uninterrupted successes already achieved in this land they were now calling New Spain. Also, it should be added, the obvious and ever-present signs of unusual wealth within Tenochtitlán had so affected the acquisitive nature of these soldier-adventurers that they were incapable of clear thought. Fascinated by evidences of wealth such as had never been encountered elsewhere in the Spanish Indies and frightened by an untenable military position the like of which Spaniards had never known previously in America, the invaders faced a moment of decision. The dilemma born of fear that would not let them stay and greed that would not permit them to go gave rise to a logical insistence that shipping be constructed for the twin purposes of intimidating the natives and aiding the invaders if eventual withdrawal became inevitable.

Up to that moment Cortés had never encountered any such problem. Aside from his experience as passenger, his nautical background merely included the acquisition of ready-built ships in Cuba and the much-disputed episode in which they were destroyed on the Vera Cruz coast. Never having built ships, Cortés laid the shipbuilding problem before his men.

First the captain general turned to individuals, among them
Bernardino Vázquez de Tapia. Failing to resolve the issue in
that manner, Cortés apparently spoke about the need for shipping
before the general company, possibly at a formal muster. Then it
was that someone mentioned Martín López as an intelligent man
whose personal servants understood the art of shipbuilding, and
Cortés hurriedly summoned the former citizen of Seville. Their
conversation about ships and shipbuilding closed with don Hernando requesting don Martín to direct the vital project.

Two decades later, when as a middle-aged citizen of Mexico
City, Martín López recalled this episode, the combination of bitter
memories and repeatedly unsuccessful litigation with Cortés had
removed the initial modesty which punctuated earlier accounts
of this chapter of his career. Then, in 1540, López bluntly said
that "Cortés . . . in trouble and prevented from continuing the
conquest, begged him to design four brigantines."[7]

In a strict sense, Martín López was not a shipwright in 1519.
Such was out of the question for a son of the knightly class in early
sixteenth-century Spain. How much experience along such lines,
if any, had been his in America prior to meeting Cortés remains
open to speculation. More likely than any direct labor on his part
is the possibility that his menservants were hired out on shipbuilding projects in the Antilles, sharpening their skills and
enriching López' purse. At any rate, López insisted in later life,
and more than one fellow conquistador testified in support of
his contention, that he was not a shipwright. Bernardino Vázquez
de Tapia, for example, asserted that López undertook the shipbuilding projects in New Spain without prior pursuit of that
trade in Castile. Gerónimo Ruiz de la Mota, a brigantine captain
during the siege of Tenochtitlán in 1521 and a longtime neighbor
of López in postwar Mexico City, claimed that López was able to
build the ships because he was ingenious and clever rather than
because of experience, for he had never been a master shipwright.

[7] López, 1529-1550, pp. 118-19, 126, Conway Coll. (LC).

Lázaro Guerrero, a fellow conquistador who had known López since about 1503 (more than a dozen years before the descendant of the Ossorios left Spain), declared López built the ships "without knowing the trade."[8]

However daring, the inexperienced do well to lean upon the experienced, and Martín López counted on the known abilities of his servants Pedro and Miguel de Mafla. Likewise he must have known that still other able workers were available, notably the toolmaker Hernán Martín, whose part was especially significant in the undertaking. When the Spaniards had plunged inland from the Vera Cruz sector of the Gulf Coast, this conquistador had come doubly armed with crossbow and blacksmith tools. Turning from ship maintenance, the blacksmith supplied shoes for the horses and arrowheads for the archers, for Cortés' cavalry and corps of infantry bowmen depended heavily upon the blacksmith's forge as long as marches were made and battles were fought. Later, blacksmith Hernán Martín stated in 1528 that "he had been present throughout and had had charge of the making of the tools for the construction of said brigantines."[9] Unlike our own day, wartime artisans of the sixteenth century have been denied the considerable credit due them.

Several other Spanish workmen joined carpenters Pedro and Miguel de Mafla, blacksmith Hernán Martín, and cousin Juan Martínez Narices in the work force of Martín López in the Aztec capital, among them Antón de Rodas and Juan Gómez de Herrera. A third carpenter was present in the person of Andrés Núñez, and another metalworker, Pedro Hernández, joined Hernán Martín. Two Spaniards, Diego Hernández and Sebastián Rodríguez, joined and supervised the Indian labor in felling trees and sawing timbers.[10] From the Indians supplied by Montezuma the Spaniards

---

[8] *Ibid.*, 118, 125, 134, 162; López, 1528-1574, p. 16, Conway Coll. (Aberdeen).

[9] López, 1528-1574, p. 14, Conway Coll. (Aberdeen).

[10] *Ibid.*, 27, 51, 54; Bernal Díaz del Castillo, *Historia verdadera de la conquista de la Nueva España*, ed. by Joaquín Ramírez Cabañas (3 vols., Mexico City, 1944), I, 386; Documents Relating to Various Suits, 78, 85, in Conway Collection (Cambridge University).

kept the real reasons for the shipbuilding program. Within four leagues of the city they found suitable oak timbers, which they cut and transported into the island metropolis.

At an appropriate moment, Cortés sent trustworthy Gonzalo de Sandoval to the coastal garrison for supplies salvaged from the Cuban ships which would serve present needs. Two heavy chains (made from the anchors and other ironwork of some of the ships destroyed on the Gulf coast), sails, tackle, pitch, tow, a mariner's compass, and other unspecified useful items were soon at the fingertips of Martín López in Tenochtitlán.[11]

In 1528, as he recounted this phase of his career in New Spain in the first of several verified statements of services he executed, Martín López asserted that the four brigantines—which had occupied him for more than five months, with each of them measuring between 25 and 26 cubits (37½ to 39 feet), dimensions corroborated by a coworker—were constructed at his own expense. López accordingly asked that he be repaid the 2,000 pesos he had spent on the undertaking. Precisely how he spent that amount on this project, if indeed he did, is not known. He could not ask that sum as wages for himself, for no one in the expedition had been promised or paid any definite amount (like other such expeditions the expectation of booty, land grants, coats of arms, and the like were hoped-for rewards). No basis for López' claim existed if he had not consumed his own treasure in the undertaking. With a later shipbuilding project, there is clear evidence that López reached into his own purse to supply his men with minor luxuries of life. It is conceivable that 1519 and Tenochtitlán saw him originate the personally financed incentive system he introduced among his workers in Tlaxcala a year later. After all, most of the Spaniards then in Tenochtitlán knew relative idleness, which must have disgruntled those who had been drafted into the work corps. Worker incentive was doubly important because of the urgency of the situation. López, with a reputation at stake in this first venture had special personal reasons, even if such included private

---

[11] Díaz del Castillo, I, 378-81.

expenditures, to insure the success of the Tenochtitlán project.

Witnesses and coworkers both agree and disagree with López regarding the amount of time spent on the four brigantines, and well might their estimates vary under conditions that counted a calendar unwanted and a diary unthought of. Alvar López, Melchor de Alabes, and Juan Ramos de Lares insisted the construction consumed about four months. In view of the fact López' shipbuilding locale speedily shifted to the Gulf coast, where he had a caravel far along toward completion before the advent of Narváez in the spring of 1520, the estimate of the above-named trio is preferred to the longer interval suggested by López himself. For a man unaccustomed both to the nature and the intensity of the work he had engaged in, however, it is easily possible López thought his labors lasted longer than was actually the case.[12] Also, it must be added, a proud and reflective conquistador easily might have later exaggerated his contribution to the common cause.

Once launched, the four brigantines constituted a naval force of significance. Each mounted a cannon in its bow and could transport seventy-five men and several horses. Their size and firepower distressed the Indians, and under a combination of sail and oar they could outrun the finest canoes of Montezuma's warriors. The four ships shook native confidence. Indian appreciation of the brigantines ripened during the episode in which Montezuma and some of his principal lords were taken on a "pleasure" trip on Lake Texcoco, a junket which introduced the Americas to European gunboat diplomacy.

The opinion entertained by the conquistadors themselves concerning the brigantines was admirably expressed by Diego Ramírez, a carpenter connected with later López projects though not a party to the construction in Tenochtitlán. Years later, Ramírez said, "because of them [the four brigantines] the Indians did not dare to rebel."[13]

---

[12] López, 1528-1574, pp. 6-7, 12, 19, 25, 54, Conway Coll. (Aberdeen).

[13] Hernán Cortés, *Cartas de relación de la conquista de Méjico* (2 vols., Madrid, 1942), I, 98; Díaz del Castillo, I, 386-87, 389-90; López, 1528-1574, p. 10, Conway Coll. (Aberdeen).

As the months thus employed passed, relations gradually
worsened between the Spaniards and their hosts. The guests,
whose prolonged stay and conduct had worn thin the hospitality
initially accorded them, had more than once wounded native
sensibilities. Repeated evidences of intolerance of Mexican religious practices irritated the followers of Montezuma. Spanish
greed for gold, seen in their loot grabbing in Tenochtitlán as well
as in the spirited reconnaissances into the mining districts, dis-
gusted their hosts. Not least among the mounting irritations was
kidnapping Montezuma and reducing him to the role of hostage.
He, in time, reported the rising temper of his countrymen and
urged Cortés to take his men and depart from the land. Indian
ruler and Spanish chieftain alike knew, however, that the Europeans had no ocean shipping in which to withdraw. Hoping to
impress the credulous Montezuma, Cortés ordered Martín López
to inaugurate another shipbuilding project, this time on the
Gulf coast.

As he set out for the slope of Mount Orizaba in the eastern
mountain range overlooking the Gulf of Mexico to continue a
career in shipbuilding, López took with him his tools and some
of the workmen, both Spanish and Indian, lately identified with
the Tenochtitlán endeavor. His assignment called for cutting the
necessary timbers and fashioning the planks and beams in the
mountain forest. Then the prepared timbers for a caravel measuring 28 cubits (42 feet) were to be transported to a site near
the garrison at Villa Rica de la Vera Cruz, where a shipyard
would be established and the assembling and launching of the
vessel effected.

The challenge this project posed for shipbuilder López is
staggering when viewed in detail. Whereas the work at Tenochtitlán made him at most a supervisor of workmen under the daily
direction of Cortés, the caravel venture found López almost on his
own, so that it can be said he had to exercise command functions.
The morale question, a minor matter at Tenochtitlán where his
workmen were constantly aware of everything that occurred, now

assumed significant proportions. Cut off from the main army, his workers, some of them not volunteers, might well feed their discontent by speculating about the booty their more fortunate colleagues back in Tenochtitlán were pocketing for themselves. There was also a real issue concerning the physical security of the isolated work party. In Tenochtitlán the workmen had known peace of mind because of the presence of their armed colleagues. With no guard force going eastward with López for the construction of the caravel, safety depended upon his diplomacy in maintaining peaceful, even cooperative, relations with the Indians. Also, the dependent Spaniards looked to the natives for food.

López demonstrated a noteworthy capacity to get along with the natives. Isolated and hard at work, he and his handful of workers wrote an early chapter in Spanish-Indian relations remarkably unlike those of Cortés, Alvarado, and others. The shipwright's cooperative endeavor and diplomacy produced a much more harmonious record than did the combination of military might and diplomacy (sometimes to be pronounced duplicity) commonly practiced by the captains of the conquest.

López also had a transportation problem of significant proportions. Once the timbers had been cut and fashioned on the slope of Mount Orizaba, they had to be moved down to the coast to a likely shipyard site. Ingenuity rather than experience had been López' chief stock in trade at Tenochtitlán, and the caravel assignment called for more of the same.

Among those accompanying López on this second project can be counted carpenters Andrés Martínez and Andrés Núñez, the latter one of the Tenochtitlán workers. Some evidence points to the presence of sawyer Diego Hernández, and logic dictates the inclusion of the shipwright's personal servants, carpenters Pedro and Miguel de Mafla, as well as cousin Juan Martínez Narices. The small number of known Spanish workmen—though, of course, others unknown to us might have been with them—can be explained variously. López might have been assigned a very small number because only a single ship was involved. A reservoir of

Spanish manpower existed within the garrison force on the coast, and it might have been intended that those Spaniards supplement the men detached from the Tenochtitlán force, especially in the assembling and launching phases. On the other hand, this small number might have been a studied effort by Cortés to postpone the completion of a ship of questionable importance to him. As long as the caravel was not ready for navigation, Cortés' argument that he could not leave the country would make sense to Montezuma. Furthermore, a small number of Spaniards would presume greater dependence upon Indian labor, which could have been the case if the experienced Indian workers at Tenochtitlán accompanied López. If, however, numerous natives of the Aztec Confederation went with López, they complicated Spanish-Indian relations even as they advanced ship construction, because the work on the caravel was performed in a region hostile to Aztec authority.

After an indeterminate period, apparently uneventful except for the hard labor entailed, the work in the woods ended with the removal of the timbers to the coast. Herein the shipwright gained valuable experience for a later and more momentous problem of overland transport. Under Spanish direction an unknown number of Indians shouldered the planking, beams, and timbers, and trudged off in the direction of Villa Rica de la Vera Cruz. Some small part of that movement eastward might have been via the waters of the Cempoala River, but even so, this phase of the caravel project was noteworthy.

The spring of 1520 saw the shipyard site established, the caravel materials on hand, and the workmen busily engaged with the tasks of ship assembly. The work, never to be completed, was far advanced when an order came from Cortés to suspend the project.

When Montejo and Puertocarrero had sailed from Vera Cruz for Spain in 1519, Cortés had ordered his couriers to bypass Cuba. Drawn by property they owned on the island, however, the two captains had touched Cuban soil momentarily, long enough for Velázquez to become aware both of the rebellion of Cortés and of the wealth of the mainland. Enraged, he at once set about equipping yet another expedition. Because it had to be big enough to cope with Cortés' force and because manpower and ships were not exactly easy to come by on Cuba after a succession of expeditions, months were required to outfit the massive venture the governor now entrusted to Narváez, the able commander who had done most in the field to win Cuba for him some years earlier.

The spring of 1520 found the Pánfilo de Narváez punitive expedition on the coast near Vera Cruz seeking an opportunity to defeat Cortés' rebels. Word of the presence of this numerous opposition—Narváez had more ships, horses, men, cannon, more of everything than did Cortés—came at an inopportune moment. The tensions which had led Montezuma, the hostage emperor, to request the speedy withdrawal of the Spaniards from his land had continued to mount. Caught between a bad situation in Tenochtitlán and a developing threat on the coast that might become even worse, the long-inactive Cortés dramatically swung into action once more. Leaving Captain Pedro de Alvarado and a Spanish garrison force of fewer than two hundred to maintain the position in the Mexican metropolis, the captain general pushed rapidly eastward with the remainder of his following.

Loyal, but outnumbered badly, the Cortés detachment grew as it neared the coast and its anticipated clash with Narváez' force. Certain Spaniards engaged in patrol and exploratory duty rejoined Cortés. The hale and hearty part of the coastal garrison commanded by Sandoval did likewise. With ships to be won, Cortés ordered Martín López and his shipbuilders to pick up their weapons and join their captain general.

In the short but decisive fighting that ensued between the two Spanish armies, López demonstrated that his fighting ability had not diminished. In the course of a confused night attack upon Narváez' position, an action wherein even the general pattern of events is far from clear, the tall shipwright distinguished himself. At just about the moment Narváez was blinded in one eye, the unusual height of Martín López enabled him to fire the thatch

of the native building in which Narváez and his principal sup-
porters had congregated. Their capture, following at once, marked
the turning point toward complete victory for Cortés' men.

Immediately Cortés added his would-be conquerors to his
following and hastened westward to Tenochtitlán. Word had
come to Cortés that relations had deteriorated between the
Spanish garrison force under Pedro de Alvarado and the natives
of the city.

Although López' unfinished 42-foot vessel did represent additional valuable experience for the shipbuilding contingent of
conquistadors, it did not involve the six months of labor López
later claimed he gave it. (It was manifestly impossible for him
to work between eleven and twelve months in the aggregate on
the brigantines and the caravel in the interval between early
November, 1519, and late June, 1520.) Years later, López claimed
his work on the caravel was worth 1,000 pesos.[14]

Once again in Tenochtitlán by late June, 1520, Cortés felt
doubly ill at ease despite the fact his Spanish following had greatly
increased. In his absence the fury of the disgruntled natives had
reached new heights. The firing of the four brigantines by the
Aztecs demonstrated Mexican fears and determination. This,
coupled with mounting Indian opposition, led Cortés to decide
that early evacuation of the city was an absolute necessity. Even
in the week between his return to Tenochtitlán and the withdrawal of June 30, Cortés again turned his attention to shipping.
Spanish efforts to raise and repair a charred and half-sunken hull,
which might have found López again in the role of artisan, were
balked by stubborn Indian opposition.

As long as the Spaniards had the vessels and resultant control
of the waters of Lake Texcoco, the position of the invaders in
Tenochtitlán had been militarily sound; the Indians recognized
this by not provoking full-fledged warfare. However, once the
brigantines were gone and retreat became necessary, the unhealthy

<hr />

[14] López, 1528-1574, pp. 7-8, 10-11, 15, 17, 19-20, 23-24, 29, 40, 46, 49,
51-52, 54, 86, Conway Coll. (Aberdeen); Díaz del Castillo, I, 422-23; II, 56-59.

position of the navyless Spaniards in the island metropolis was spelled out in the greatest losses ever suffered by such a large, well-armed Spanish force in all the years of New World conquest.

Now, Cortés' projected plan of retreat called for still more artisan activity. Planning a speedy, unheralded, nighttime withdrawal from the city, Cortés recognized as bottlenecks the numerous removable bridges on the short western (Tacuba) causeway which he had chosen for the exit route. Especially important to the safe passage of the horsemen and the artillery was a portable bridge which Cortés ordered built those last days in Tenochtitlán. Cortés would have done well, had circumstances permitted, to build as many bridges as there were potential waterholes. Failure to do so added to the costly casualty rate he sustained in a few rain-drenched hours of furious fighting that night of June 30–July 1, 1520.

On that occasion, recorded as the Sad Night, Cortés lost every piece of his artillery, possibly 70 percent of his horses, and approximately 65 percent of his total Spanish force. Failure to maintain control of the brigantines and failure to increase the number of portable bridges accounted for a considerable measure of the calamity that befell the Spaniards. Complicated, too, would be future activity by workers who had been forced to abandon their tools during that nightmarish withdrawal. Blacksmith Hernán Martín, to save his life, had discarded his forge and tools valued at 1,000 pesos.[15]

After the weary and wounded survivors had dragged themselves onto the mainland at the west side of Lake Texcoco, a depressed captain general checked his losses and in so doing hinted at his future course of action. Hearing that approximately eight hundred of his men were dead, Cortés asked specifically only about one individual, Martín López, and was very pleased to learn López was among the living.[16]

The work that lay ahead for Martín López and the germ of the

[15] Información de Hernán Martín (1531), Paso y Troncoso Coll., Leg. 95.
[16] Gardiner, 89.

plans of reconquest Cortés was formulating even then were sensed by Bernardino Vázquez de Tapia in his words: "this witness is of the opinion that Our Lord inspired him [Cortés] to believe that by means of this Martín López the city would be regained which they had now lost."[17]

[17] López, 1529-1550, p. 130, Conway Coll. (LC); Francisco Cervantes de Salazar, *Crónica de la Nueva España* (Madrid, 1914), 493.

# CHAPTER III

# A WORKER-WARRIOR IN VICTORY

HE BATTERED survivors of that night of catastrophe on the causeways marched and fought their way toward Tlaxcala, homeland of the still faithful Indian allies. There, for most of July, the wounded Spanish warriors demonstrated their remarkable recuperative powers—and soon enough men were available to carry out the plans their leader had in mind.[1]

Mustering his able-bodied followers, a group that counted Martín López, who had recovered from his four wounds, Cortés led them southeast on what is termed the Tepeaca campaign. That unbroken string of victories which began in midsummer and continued down to the Christmas season had multisided importance: it boosted Spanish morale; it assured a line of communication with the coast (the founding of the garrison at Segura de la Frontera was the clincher); and it permitted Cortés to start unraveling his scheme of combined operations for the reconquest of the Valley of Mexico.

One day at Tepeaca, Cortés instructed López: "Proceed to the city of Tlaxcala with your tools and everything necessary and seek for a place where you can cut much wood—oak, evergreen oak, and pine—and fashion it into the pieces necessary to build thirteen brigantines."[2] The orders which sent the shipwright and a number of artisans to Tlaxcala for his third shipbuilding project were given wide publicity by the captain general, quite possibly at a general muster. To encourage his troops, too many of whom wished to evacuate New Spain, and to encourage reluctant workers, some of whom went unwillingly with López, Cortés must have sketched, at least in broad outline, the army-navy siege technique he planned to employ against Tenochtitlán.

Of the fourteen Spanish workmen who can be identified among the shipbuilders in Tlaxcala, seven were carpenters, one a blacksmith, one a specialist in calking vessels, and five laborers of miscellaneous types. Four of the carpenters—one of the Maflas, Diego Hernández, Andrés Martínez, and Andrés López—had been with the shipwright on either one or both of the prior projects, and the remaining three, Diego Ramírez, Alvar López, and Francisco Rodríguez, were additions to his work force. The blacksmith, none other than Hernán Martín, brought much New World experience with him, as did calker Juan Gómez de Herrera. Among the workers whose trades were not named were cousin Juan Martínez Narices (for the third time), Lázaro Guerrero (who did some catering when he was not carpentering), Clemente de Barcelona, Antón de Rodas (for a second time), and Pablo del Retamal.

Prior to setting out, the shipwright purchased a quantity of supplies. Mystery attends their amount and nature, but not the use to which they were put. In the words of the self-confident

1 Detailed treatment of the brigantine-construction activities of Martín López, the land campaigns of Cortés, and the combined army-navy operations against Tenochtitlán is in Gardiner, *Naval Power*, 86-185.

2 López, 1528-1574, pp. 4-5, Conway Coll. (Aberdeen).

sawyer Diego Hernández, "Martín López purchased and sent to Tlaxcala, where the said timber was to be cut, wine and vinegar and oil, which he shared with this witness and the other men who were helping in the work on the timber." Another worker, Francisco Rodríguez, added cheese and native clothing to the list of items furnished by the shipwright. A third worker in Tlaxcala, Clemente de Barcelona, indicated López acquired the supplies from Vera Cruz.[3]

The provisions supplied at his own expense give a key to the nature of López and to the situation he and his men faced. An energetic man who was expected to produce within a few months time about as many ships as he had Spanish workers at his disposal would be inclined, with his own reputation also at stake, to put his all into the undertaking. It is evident, too, that López was naturally generous; the supplies furnished his workers in Tlaxcala were but the latest in a series of demonstrations of this generosity.

His base was the city of Tlaxcala, but López led his men into the forests on the nearby slopes of Mount Malinche. There selected trees were felled and future ships' timbers given a preliminary dressing before Indian bearers shouldered them for the downhill trip to the bank of the Zahuapan River a short distance above the city of Tlaxcala. Some confusion attends the exact amount of the work done on the timbers in the forests because of variations in statements made by the shipwright on different occasions.[4]

Eyewitness accounts of numerous workers indicate Martín López was something more than mere designer-supervisor. His own statement that while in Tlaxcala he was "doing the labor of two skilled men" might be discounted seriously were it not that every one of the ten witnesses he later presented in his behalf gave testimony in support of his assertion. Carpenter Alvar López put it pointedly when he said, "Martín López never rested until the brigantines were completed, directing the work and doing

---

[3] *Ibid.*, 38-39, 41-42, 48, 58-59.
[4] *Ibid.*, 5; López, 1529-1550, p. 120, Conway Coll. (LC).

much of it himself." Fellow worker Lázaro Guerrero "had
observed how diligently he [the shipwright] toiled in everything
connected with their construction, all day long, and often after
dark and before dawn by the aid of candles, working himself and
directing and encouraging the other workmen, with the zeal of
a man who comprehended the urgency of the matter."[5] Before
the Christmas season of 1520, and with it the return of Cortés and
his men briefly to Tlaxcala, most, if not all, of the ships' timbers
had been assembled near the waters of the Zahuapan.

Meanwhile, Cortés and his field force had known successes and
received reinforcements. During the weeks that followed the
shipbuilders' departure from Tepeaca, a combination of circumstances brought successive shiploads of men to the coast of New
Spain, almost all of whom were incorporated into Cortés' force.
In late 1520 six ships, about 175 men, a score of horses, and
indeterminate quantities of much-needed food and military supplies arrived. Ships' gear and masters and seamen enriched the
future navy under way in the hill country of Tlaxcala.

After swinging westward and pushing to the southeastern corner
of the mountain rim fringing the Valley of Mexico, Cortés con-
solidated his position between that point and the coast by establishing a permanent garrison at Segura de la Frontera and winning
the Cholulans to his side. Then he revisited Tlaxcala.

A personal check on the status of the shipbuilding project led
Cortés to send to the coast for nails, iron, sails, tackle, and other
gear needed to complete the brigantines. He ordered all blacksmiths still on the coast to Tlaxcala, and he also dispatched four
sailors into nearby pine woods to obtain pitch for calking. Cortés
won renewed pledges of cooperation from the principal Tlaxcalan
chieftains, with special support promised the brigantine project.

Foot soldier Bernal Díaz, long since having concluded "that
we could never master the lake without sloops," spoke of the
brigantines and their designer-builder with evident affection.

    [5] López, 1528-1574, pp. 58, 66-67, 76, 85, 94, 102, 110, 118, 125, 131, 138,
Conway Coll. (Aberdeen).

"Martín López made such speed in cutting the wood with the great assistance rendered him by the Indians, that he had the whole of it cut within a few days, and each beam marked for the position for which it was intended to occupy, after the manner that the master carpenters and boat builders have of marking it." Writing many years after the events, Bernal Díaz signified Martín López' importance to Spanish purposes, as of 1520, in these words: "It seems to me, that if some ill luck had prevented his being one of the first to come in our company, we might have wasted much time." Cortés' appraisal of shipwright and shipbuilders, in Tepeaca, Tlaxcala, and subsequently in the city of Texcoco, is seen in workman Diego Ramírez' words that "he had been one of those present when don Hernando Cortés threw his arms round Martín López and the other workmen on the brigantines, . . . telling them that they were worth their weight in gold and that he would see that they were better rewarded than any others."[6]

Cortés now had the courage to reinvade the Valley of Mexico, a courage born of victories, reinforcements, and knowledge that his naval arm would be ready by the time his army campaign in the Valley of Mexico readied the siege of Tenochtitlán itself. Two days after Christmas, Cortés mustered his field force, left Tlaxcala, and proceeded toward the populous city of Texcoco, the base he had elected within the valley several leagues due east across the lake from Tenochtitlán. Left behind in Tlaxcala was shipwright Martín López with his corps of Spanish workers, his Indian assistants, and a job to finish.

Early 1521 witnessed the assembling and testing of the brigantines on the Zahuapan River several kilometers above the city of Tlaxcala. Since it was the dry season, a dam had to be built to impound sufficient water to test the ships. Once they were proved generally satisfactory, López dismantled the brigantines for the herculean task ahead, that of transporting this prefabricated navy

[6] Bernal Díaz del Castillo, *The True History of the Conquest of New Spain*, tr. and ed. by Alfred Percival Maudslay, Hakluyt Society ser. 2, XXIII-XXV, XXX, XL (5 vols., London, 1908-1916), II, 300-302; López, 1528-1574, pp. 9, 18, 22, Conway Coll. (Aberdeen).

to the Valley of Mexico and the scene of its eventual use. Twelve
of the vessels measured between 27 and 28 cubits (40½ to 42 feet)
in length, while the larger thirteenth vessel, planned as the flagship, was 32 cubits (48 feet) long. Their construction and original
assembly represented a mammoth undertaking, and their transportation, timber by timber, over more than fifty miles of rolling
and mountainous terrain was also a memorable part of the miracle
engineered by Martín López.

Before the siege of Tenochtitlán could begin, the navy had to
be completed and the position of the ground forces in the valley
strengthened. The first five months of 1521 found the ground
forces busy. The Spanish widened the area controlled by Cortés
from his base on the eastern shore of Lake Texcoco, and promoted
alliances between the invaders and certain communities previously
loyal to Aztec authority. They also sent out forces for reconnaissance and procurement of supplies. The names of such leaders as
Sandoval, Alvarado, and Olid, and the names of such places as
Iztapalapa and Chalco often were written into the record of the
early months of 1521.

Sometime about mid-February, Sandoval was sent eastward
with twin objectives: to punish a recalcitrant Indian community
and to escort the brigantine materials into Texcoco. Meanwhile,
Martín López and such Tlaxcalan chieftains as Chichimecatecle,
Ayotecatl, and Teuctepil already had begun to move the brigantines westward. Tens of thousands of Tlaxcalans were assigned
to transport the knocked-down ships, to carry foodstuffs for the
caravan, or to guard the prized timbers. For many miles within
the province of Tlaxcala, the shipwright and the native chieftains
directed the antlike overland progress of the future navy. Near
the Tlaxcalan frontier, advance elements from Sandoval's detachment encountered the caravan. Still nearer Texcoco, Sandoval
himself met and assumed direction of this strange expedition.

The huge caravan embraced more than 50,000 men, stretched
out over a distance of more than two leagues, and required six
hours to pass a given point. Out in front Sandoval placed 8 Span-

ish horsemen, 100 Spanish infantrymen, and 10,000 Tlaxcalan warriors. Immediately behind that vanguard came 8,000 native porters with the knocked-down vessels and 2,000 native porters with the food supply needed for the trip from Tlaxcala to Texcoco. Behind the core of the caravan came a rearguard of 7 Spanish horsemen, 100 Spanish infantrymen, and 10,000 Tlaxcalan fighters. Along each of the extended flanks of the heart of the caravan marched 10,000 more native warriors.

Four days after Sandoval assumed command, the caravan made its triumphal entry into Texcoco with everyone in his finest apparel for the moment of joyous welcome. Surely Martín López dressed for the festivities which saw trumpeters and drummers and happy Spaniards, led by Cortés himself, come out to usher the brigantines into the city. Cortés gave copious thanks to the Tlaxcalan chieftains, but there is no record he conferred the same attention and honor upon his indispensable shipwright. Having already said, "Build these brigantines and I will pay you in a way that will more than satisfy you," the captain general possibly thought it unnecessary to compliment López on this occasion.[7]

Texcoco became increasingly the center of multiple activities. More reinforcements arrived and were integrated into the Spanish force; there was more campaigning and the final assembling and launching of the brigantines.

The shipyard was established along a narrow, shallow stream bed approximately a half league from the lake, and the months of March and April, 1521, saw the naval project pushed on two fronts simultaneously, for a canal had to be dug while the ships were being readied. The canal, measuring 12 feet wide and 12 feet deep, was entirely an Indian triumph, as 40,000 Texcocans, in relays of 8,000 men each, toiled more than a month and a half under the general direction of Texcocan chieftain Ixtlilxochitl.

Control of the lake rested with the natives and their tens of thousands of canoes, and the brigantines could not be assembled

[7] Cortés, *Cartas de relación*, I, 195-96; Díaz del Castillo, *Historia verdadera*, II, 164-66; López, 1528-1574, pp. 4-6, Conway Coll. (Aberdeen).

on the lakefront, because Cortés could not spare the men to guard them. Cortés therefore had to tell Martín López to establish the shipyard inland and then order digging of the canal. Despite the inland construction program, the ships still were the objects of several serious but unsuccessful sabotage efforts by the worried Mexicans. Cortés had laid his plans so that three activities would be concluded almost simultaneously: the mopping-up and final reconnaissance in the valley, completion of the canal by Ixtlilxochitl, and the assembling of the ships by López. Then all would be ready for the combined land and lake effort against Tenochtitlán.

A clear and detailed picture of the final work on the brigantines, amid the bustle of last-minute preparations of so many kinds, cannot be traced. Most of the men who worked with the shipwright in Tlaxcala continued with the ships in Texcoco. In addition, some other artisans were added to the Spanish work force, among them Melchor de Alabes, Juan Ramos de Lares, and Antón Cordero. Blacksmiths Hernando Aguilar, Hernando Alonso, and Juan García made many of the metallic items needed those last moments in Texcoco. The ubiquitous blacksmith Hernán Martín turned aside from the brigantines to produce a gigantic stockpile of 120,000 arrowheads for the forthcoming Battle of Tenochtitlán.[8]

By the last week of April the López-directed project was so advanced that launching was eagerly awaited. The final touches involved particularly careful and thorough calking of all seams, erection of the masts, fitting of sails, and the mounting of a cannon in the bow of each vessel.

On the last Sunday of April the ships slipped through the canal into the lake, ready for battle. Fray Olmedo celebrated a mass and blessed the fleet before a throng of Spaniards and native allies.

---

[8] López, 1528-1574, pp. 18, 25, 102, Conway Coll. (Aberdeen); Díaz del Castillo, *Historia verdadera*, II, 165-66; G. R. G. Conway, "Hernando Alonso, a Jewish Conquistador with Cortés in Mexico," *Publications of the American Jewish Historical Society*, XXXI (1928), 11, 12, 25; Información de los méritos y servicios de Juan García (1550), Paso y Troncoso Coll., Leg. 94; Información de Hernán Martín (1531), *ibid.*, Leg. 95.

Cortés then mustered his manpower and assigned the men to specific divisions.

May, 1521, saw the ships, their masters, and their complements of gunners, archers, and paddlers welded into an effective fighting force. Cortés assigned more than 300 men, a third of his total Spanish force, to the thirteen vessels. Each ship had a complement of twenty-five, of whom a dozen were paddlers (six on each side) and an equal number of gunners and bowmen. Special emphasis on the navy is seen in the fact that Cortés assigned captains and crews for the naval units before he composed the three land divisions of Alvarado, Olid, and Sandoval. The navy had twice as much Spanish manpower as any one land division. Of such specialized fighters as crossbowmen and musketeers, the navy had from half to three-quarters of the total Spanish strength. Of a total of eighteen cannon, the navy carried fourteen, the flagship being distinguished with two pieces of ordnance. The firepower of the navy and its special kind of mobility caused captain general and common foot soldier alike to term this newly created force "the key of the whole war."

In the distribution of manpower, shipwright Martín López became an officer aboard the flagship *La Capitana*.[9] Those days of May, 1521, were marked by movements of the brigantines in eastern waters of Lake Texcoco to coordinate paddle and sail, and the movements of the fleet as a unit—those movements intended as shakedown cruises for a green navy.

The lines of the brigantines resembled the better known caravels and galleons of the period, with high castles at bow and stern separated by a longer well-decked midsection. On the forward castle was mounted a cannon, and nearby stood the mud pilot so necessary for successful navigation in shallow lake waters. There, too, in time of battle a gunner or crossbowman might be found. Amidships, in the ship's well, arose the mast from which hung the square-rigged sail. Along the gunwales of the low midsection stood the paddlers, who in moments of conflict doubled as warriors

[9] López, 1528-1574, p. 62, Conway Coll. (Aberdeen).

with guns and bows and lances. The square stern, designed in part to give added stability to the nearly flat-bottomed craft, afforded another platform area for fighting men as well as the strong-armed rudder tender. Towering over the slower native canoes—and powerful enough to crush them in ramming tactics—the wide-beamed, shallow-draught brigantines enabled the Spaniards to wage eye-level warfare with the Mexicans astride the causeways.

Before the end of May, Cortés initiated the strategy which combined elements of blockade, siege, and assault. In counter-clockwise march the divisions of Alvarado and Olid went to their respective posts in the lakefront communities of Tacuba and Coyoacán on the western side of Lake Texcoco. Once in place, and having broken the aqueduct which supplied Tenochtitlán with fresh water, Alvarado and Olid were poised and ready to begin fighting on the causeways leading toward that metropolis. Then Sandoval left Texcoco and skirted the southern shore of that lake, moving westward against Iztapalapa and the southernmost causeway. The last day of May, Cortés went aboard the flagship, and with the movement westward of the navy, the Battle of Tenochtitlán was inaugurated.

For seventy-five days thereafter, until the calm of August 13 signaled final victory for the invaders, every man under Cortés, Spaniard and Indian alike, rose to well-nigh incomprehensible heights of endurance and courage and endeavor. In the climactic struggle involving hundreds of thousands of combatants, scant attention has been paid the contribution of the individual; here we shall view those last days of Aztec power in the island metropolis through the personal performance of Martín López.

Moving to support Sandoval's operation against Iztapalapa, the fleet turned aside momentarily to assault an Indian position atop a rocky island hillock. While half the manpower of the Spanish navy stormed ashore, officer López, serving as pilot major of the entire fleet, remained afloat.[10] The landing party barely had

---

[10] Cervantes de Salazar, *Crónica de la Nueva España*, 646, 659, 699.

tasted victory when it was ordered to reembark so that the fleet could move to face the threat posed by the approach of thousands of Aztec canoes crowded with warriors.

In this unique fleet action the López-built creations spread destruction among the Mexican canoes. In a brilliant victory the brigantines pursued the remnants of Aztec power to the waterways of the city proper, and control of the lake waters passed to Spanish hands. The invaders tried to follow up with complete annihilation of the lake-surface power of the defenders. In headlong pursuit *La Capitana* led the brigantines up against the perimeter of the city, where the flagship became stranded in the shallow water.

It was a moment of crisis. As hordes of enemy natives closed in upon the grounded vessel, Commander in Chief Juan Rodríguez de Villafuerte abandoned ship, with most of the crew emulating his ignoble example. From López, however, the crisis drew forth desperate courage. He took charge of the small remaining group of loyal crewmen to defend the vessel. Grasping sword and shield, he led the fight to clear the ship of the enemy who already had boarded it. That done, he seized a crossbow and struck down the leader of the enemy contingent. As the leaderless Aztec force withdrew, López and his faithful few refloated the stranded ship and moved once more into deeper waters.

All who witnessed this demonstration of valor and leadership by López united in praise of his heroism. Men of the crew of *La Capitana* exclaimed they owed their lives to López; men aboard other ships of the fleet marveled at the nature and measure of his heroic action. Beyond the importance inherent in the salvage of the ship and the rescue of his shipmates was the morale factor of López' contribution. Antón Cordero, who saw it all from the brigantine in which he was serving, said, "had the Indians succeeded in taking the vessel they would have been encouraged and the Christians correspondingly disheartened."[11] Thus, on the very first day of fighting, Martín López not only

[11] López, 1528-1574, pp. 62, 71, 80, 90, 97-98, 106, 114, 134, Conway Coll. (Aberdeen); López, 1529-1550, pp. 122-23, 130-31, 138, Conway Coll. (LC).

contributed notably to the victory but also to the continuance of the psychological advantage the brigantines gave the Spaniards. By the spring of 1521 the Mexicans had faced sword, crossbow, lance, arquebus, cannon, and horse so frequently that these weapons no longer combined the psychological advantage of novelty with the physical power advantage they represented. The brigantines alone had undiminished psychological import, and Martín López enabled them to maintain that advantage longer by virtue of his salvage of the flagship on May 31. There is strong reason to believe that the man promoted so dramatically by the stress of battle to the role of master continued to command the flagship during the remainder of the lake warfare.

Naval action of the opening day of conflict produced an astonishing measure of success and thus rewrote the subsequent plan of battle. Instead of going to the support of Sandoval's division after the affair of the rocky island hillock, the fleet's victory enabled Cortés to effect a landing at Acachinanco, junction of the Coyoacán and Iztapalapa causeways. This amphibious operation, allowing Cortés to establish his base at Acachinanco, beyond the midpoint between the mainland and the city, permitted both Olid from Coyoacán and Sandoval from Iztapalapa to make more rapid advances than otherwise would have been possible along those causeways.

Subsequent days and weeks of bitter fighting demonstrated the soundness of the concept of combined operations upon which Cortés had based his land-lake strategy. When critical supplies, such as gunpowder, had to be transferred from one division to another, the brigantines did the job. When ground forces wanted to effect behind-the-lines landings, the brigantines moved the men. With infantry thrusts in progress along the causeway, added momentum was generated and greater gain registered because of the aid and protection the brigantines gave the flanks of the ground troops. At large waterholes brigantines ran into the openings and formed the equivalent of pontoon bridges for the ground forces. When Cortés saw how brigantine support of his personally led drives on the southern causeway effected a more rapid advance than the navyless efforts of Alvarado from the west and Sandoval from the north (sent there when the captain general took charge of the southern front), he wisely divided his navy among his land commanders. Throughout the fighting of the middle months of 1521 the brigantines applied the most relentless blockade against the city of Tenochtitlán.

In this brigantine activity emerges another performance of Martín López. On one occasion López and *La Capitana* were leading a brigantine squadron, supported by friendly Indian canoes, on a raid against the very heart of Venice-like Tenochtitlán. Cautiously they made their way through the major waterways in the vicinity of the giant plaza dominating the center of the city. Grasping the royal standard carried by the flagship, López jumped ashore and personally led the thrust into the plaza area. As the detachment reached that innermost part of the Mexican stronghold, López held the Spanish flag aloft and cried out, "Victory, victory for the King of Spain." Colleagues stated that thereafter the Spaniards could enter the area freely and without fear. Evident is the truth of the declaration, "He was always first in battle and first to enter difficult places."[12]

Finally, on August 13, 1521, with the capture of Cuauhtémoc, the last of the Aztec rulers, stillness came over the blood-drenched city. The nerve center of the native culture was prostrate. Defeated natives had to continue to fight, this time against starvation. Victorious Spaniards, even as they withdrew momentarily to Coyoacán on the southwest shore of the lake and planned a new city on the site of rubble-strewn Tenochtitlán, were beset by the uncertainties that faced a victor even in sixteenth-century America. At this moment a conquistador who had turned artisan and then had served as ship captain returned to the ranks of the army. Martín López became just another soldier once more, standing watches and undoubtedly wondering, as he did so, whether the victory in the valley had ended a war or merely a phase thereof.[13]

[12] López, 1529-1550, pp. 119, 123, 131, 138-39, 146, 153, 160, 166-67, Conway Coll. (LC).
[13] *Ibid.*, 55.

# CHAPTER IV

# MEN AND MATTERS IN TRANSITION

THE SPANISH victory at Tenochtitlán marked the end of one phase of military conquest and the beginning of the cultural conquest of New Spain. For the decade from the capture of Cuauhtémoc to the arrival of the second *audiencia*, New Spain was host to confused transition.

Those were years when full-time soldiers became part-time soldiers or reverted entirely to civilian life. The all-powerful Cortés saw his authority repeatedly curtailed as one royal official after another arrived on the scene. The sharp edge of the sword was challenged by the scribe, the notary, the relator. The masculine tone of early years of conquest yielded to settled family life as men brought to the new land women left behind in the islands or in Spain, or married ones they had come to love among the natives. Friendships flourished and enmities deepened. Military life gave way to social hierarchy. The bishop buttressed the work of the itinerant friar. Those were decisive years, when every Spaniard on the continent, lesser figures like Martín López as well as the chieftains who dominate the historical record, helped in the widening Hispanization of New World life.

Few cities have known more desolation than Tenochtitlán on August 13, 1521. The invading Spaniards had safeguarded their advances by razing the buildings which fell into their hands, with the rubble consigned to the watercourses and lake proper. By the time this stone-by-stone leveling of the Aztec capital had reached the core of its architectural grandeur, Tenochtitlán was in a desperate plight. The civilian population was reduced to starvation. Disease, death, and putrefaction were on all sides when finally Tenochtitlán fell; both victor and vanquished momentarily deserted the once-proud island metropolis, now unfit for human habitation.

Leaderless and homeless, the battered, starving defenders stumbled over the causeways to the mainland, there to grovel for food. Dazed and degraded, they awaited the orders of their new masters. Meanwhile, Cortés had led the Spaniards to the community of Coyoacán on the southwest side of Lake Texcoco. There blacksmith Hernán Martín produced eleven pieces of ordnance and made the tools that fashioned some of the metallic pieces Cortés sent to the crown.[1]

It was from Coyoacán that Cortés finally decided that the seat of Spanish authority should be on the site of old Tenochtitlán, taking a cue from the priestly practice of raising crosses on the exact sites of old sacrificial stones. Aware, too, of the minority position of the victors, Cortés must have had strategic reasons as well for choosing the island position.

The Mexicans soon were subjected to further humiliation, for the abject Indians were required to complete the destruction of every architectural monument in the ruined city that might continue to remind them of their cultural heritage.

[1] Información de Hernán Martín (1531), Paso y Troncoso Coll., Leg. 95.

Only when old Tenochtitlán had given way to a newly erected Spanish-style community did Cortés permit his followers to move from Coyoacán to infant Mexico City. Indian labor produced the first church and earliest public buildings fronting on the customary plaza. Indian labor erected housing and laid streets in the usual rectangular patterns. Indian labor built the arsenal into which the brigantines were moved. The town council which had begun to function in Coyoacán transferred itself to the new municipality. By the tens of thousands the natives were permitted to return to certain quarters of the new capital. To the Spanish conquistadors were granted building lots and garden plots as supplements to the already pocketed booty.

One day late in 1521 Hernando Cortés, based in Coyoacán, distributed the booty from Tenochtitlán, and in so doing, unleashed a wave of resentment that colored subsequent decades of Spanish activity in New Spain. A truly royal portion was set aside for the crown, and to Cortés went a princely share. The remainder, a not too considerable amount, thanks to the failure of many to deposit in the common treasury choice items they had acquired, was divided among hundreds of Spaniards. That day some men learned their three years of service and hardship merited as little as sixty pesos reward.[2]

An enemy of the former shipwright asserted, in 1529, that Martín López "received four hundred pesos, the same as the commanders Pedro de Alvarado and Gonzalo de Sandoval and Cristóbal de Olid, the most prominent leaders of the army, for which four hundred pesos he gave his written acknowledgment."[3] If such be true—and that information was unchallenged in a case wherein many statements were under fire—López was honored in being grouped with the trio of famous land captains. But the shipwright who received four hundred pesos was as displeased with his share of the booty as was sawyer Diego Hernández, allotted sixty pesos. Their common disgruntlement later inspired similar courses of action.

[2] Docs. Various Suits, 87, Conway Coll. (Cambridge).
[3] López, 1529-1550, pp. 20-21, Conway Coll. (LC).

The inequitable booty distribution caused many men to move irrevocably toward enmity for Cortés. Not unrepresentative were the views of Diego Hernández and Andrés García when they charged that Cortés "had taken for himself all of the gold and jewelry."[4] The booty distribution helped to undermine the equalitarian camaraderie of the early period of the military conquest. Many a battle-weary Spaniard realized he could not yet stop and enjoy the life of a gentleman, and so constituted manpower for the continuing military operations. Possibly Cortés had paid his men so poorly in order to force them to continue their military service. If the captain general so reasoned, he failed to consider the difficulty of controlling the discontented.

The booty distribution also aroused ill will among men of the various divisions. The land divisions had failed to round up much treasure in the closing days of the Battle of Tenochtitlán, and it was charged that the men in naval service had made off with the loot. In the case of López this general condemnation of the navy gave way to the specific charge that he "as master of one of the brigantines . . . participated in the looting and obtained a large quantity of gold pesos and jewels and attire and other things to the value of two thousand pesos in gold, more or less, for which he was not held to account as he did not report them."[5]

As men came to dislike Cortés, they directed more and more of their strong personal loyalty to the captains with whom they began ranging over the outer limits of the Aztec domain. In the first years this decentralization of loyalties contributed to the concept of regional caudillos that so plagued Spanish America in later centuries.

After a brief respite, Cortés once more put a number of expeditionary forces into the field. Though significant in the total conquest of Mexico, these lesser victories compete unsuccessfully with the more dramatic earlier one for a place in the pages of history. Now more administrator than soldier, Cortés remained in the Valley of Mexico as he directed the movements of men pushing the frontiers of Spanish authority farther north and west

---

[4] Docs. Various Suits, 79, 80, Conway Coll. (Cambridge).
[5] López, 1529-1550, pp. 20-21, 50, Conway Coll. (LC).

and south from that growing seat of power. To Pánuco on the
Gulf, to Jalisco and the Chichimeca frontier on the north, to
Colima and Zacatula and Tehuantepec on the Pacific, and overland to Guatemala and juncture with Spanish forces moving
northward through Central America from Panama—to all these
points and more, mere handfuls of fighting men transmitted
Spanish authority. No man marched on even a majority of those
expeditions, but possibly very few men failed to march on at
least some of them.

Francisco de Orozco with a small detachment pushed southward
from the fortress of Segura de la Frontera into the region of
Oaxaca. Gonzalo de Sandoval, with more than two hundred
Spaniards and an unknown number of Indian allies, left the
Valley of Mexico in October, 1521, for Tuxtepec and the Gulf
coast to the south of Vera Cruz. Charged with widening Spanish
authority and locating a site for a better Gulf-coast port, Sandoval
was most fortunately situated at the moment the first royal
challenge to Cortés' control of New Spain occurred.

Vested with authority as royal governor, Cristóbal de Tapia, a
long-term servant of the crown in the Antilles, suddenly appeared
at Vera Cruz one day early in December, 1521. With Cortés and
his following still hopeful that their numerous petitions to Spain
would inspire the crown to confer authority upon them in this
land they had added to the patrimony of the king, Tapia met
delays and opposition that prevented his carrying out his assignment to displace Cortés. Spokesmen from the four municipalities
of Mexico City, Vera Cruz, Segura de la Frontera, and Medellín,
the last-named of which had just been established by Sandoval,
petitioned his departure. The military might of Sandoval proved
downright menacing. By early January, 1522, the would-be governor had been encouraged to return to the Antilles.

With this threat past, Cortés, lured on by rumor and reconnaissance, sent a force under Captain Cristóbal de Olid and onetime naval commander Juan Rodríguez de Villafuerte westward
into the Tarascan country of Michoacán, beyond which Rodríguez

de Villafuerte quickly pushed to the Pacific coast. Simultaneously Pedro de Alvarado marched southward with about three hundred Spaniards to inaugurate the Tututepeque campaigning which eventually led him to Guatemala. Having played his role of protector of Cortés' interests at Vera Cruz in the Tapia episode, Sandoval resumed the Gulf-coast penetration which by mid-1522 found him establishing the town of Espíritu Santo.

These expeditions of 1522 were succeeded by others in the months that immediately followed, expeditions which penetrated Colima on the Pacific and Pánuco on the Gulf as well as more distant areas of the isthmus of Tehuantepec. Sometimes a particularly stubborn native opposition called forth more than one Spanish effort. Invariably, although some of the wanderers elected to stay in newly conquered regions, serving as first citizens for such Spanish towns as Zacatula, Colima, and San Estevan del Puerto, many of the weary warriors returned to Mexico City.

Like so many others in the dimly recorded thirty months following the fall of Tenochtitlán, Martín López spent some time in the Valley of Mexico and some time away from it. Nothing is known of any contributions he might have made to the initial construction of Mexico City. Nor is it clear that he participated in any of the earliest expeditions that fanned out in almost every direction. From hazy references to Martín López' identification with post-Tenochtitlán conquests, we learn that on a number of occasions he enjoyed minor command responsibilities, charged by Cortés with the administration of expenditures.[6] There is no evidence such duty enriched him in the least, though once more the possibility of quietly pocketed personal loot should not be discounted. One instance found him pushing into Pánuco as one of the fifty horsemen in the column led by Gonzalo de Sandoval in the campaign of 1523-1524.[7] This trip to the Gulf coast, as a horseman, was made in finer style than the previous army duty

[6] *Ibid.*, 123, 131, 139, 146-47, 153, 160, 167.
[7] López, 1528-1574, pp. 63, 72, 99, 141, Conway Coll. (Aberdeen); Cortés, *Cartas de relación* II, 99.

which had found him a mere foot soldier. The transition by López from trudging infantryman to cavalryman was commonplace among the conquistadors in the post-Tenochtitlán campaigning. It implies two things: the continued introduction of horses into the land from the Caribbean islands, and sums of money for their purchase which so exceeded the booty shares that it is plainly evident that not all the loot had entered the common treasury of the expedition. As is true of the other conquistadors, the financial position of the former shipwright in the early 1520's cannot be clearly established.

For half a decade after this duty in the pacification of Pánuco—until the close of the 1520's—there is no additional evidence that López served in any military capacity. Perhaps he was by nature more civilian than soldier—his earlier military career had marked him more worker than warrior—and if such be so, he must have spent most of the tumultuous twenties in Mexico City itself.

More important than niggardly shares of booty or building lots or gardening plots in supporting the conquistadors in varying degrees of dignity were the grants of *encomiendas* made to them, grants whereby Spaniards either received annual tribute in money and goods from assigned groups of natives or possessed legal right to their services. Precisely when the first encomiendas were granted in New Spain is open to question. However, their significance as a principal area of continuing cultural contact between native and invader is clear and certain.

On one of those unknown occasions when encomiendas were assigned as partial payment for the services of the volunteer soldiers, Martín López received half of the pueblo of Tequixquiac. Sharing that community as fellow *encomendero* was none other than his long-term acquaintance and fellow brigantine-builder, carpenter Andrés Núñez.

Within the present state of Mexico, this old Indian community, which is thought to have been founded by a tribe of the Chichimecas in 1168, lies some fifty-five kilometers due north of Mexico City. Situated on the slopes of a barranca, Tequixquiac occupied land broken by various small hills which gradually descended to the plains of Atitalaquia. In modern times the region has attracted attention largely through its selection as the zone through which the drainage system for the Valley of Mexico passed, an engineering feat which included a tunnel at Tequixquiac.

From earliest Spanish contacts with the area, the pueblo of Tequixquiac had served as the administrative seat of the municipality of the same name within the district of Zumpango. Close to the northern end of the Valley of Mexico, Tequixquiac was high and cold, with frosts interfering with efforts to raise crops. Among the inhabitants the Spaniards found there the Otomí language predominated, with some Nahuatl also used. In pre-Hispanic days the district in which Tequixquiac lay paid its tribute in mantles and weapons.

Without the document which conferred this encomienda upon Martín López, speculation attends certain matters. The number of Indians involved is unknown, but with the land far from among the most attractive of the valley, it is expected they were not particularly numerous. An indirect index to their number, as well as to their economic capacity, is contained in López' statement late in 1534 (incidentally, his first direct mention of the grant) that the encomienda was "one of the smallest and poorest in the land, not being worth one hundred pesos." The precise terms of the payment of the tribute to the encomendero are also uncertain. Unrelated as it was to the numerous mining districts, one suspects the tribute was paid in the crops and goods customarily encountered in the preconquest tribute lists. Obviously an encomienda which yielded an annual income of less than one hundred pesos to its Spanish master must have involved small numbers of Indians and inferior terrain. The poverty of the district and the smallness of the grant combine to mark Martín López' encomienda as particularly insignificant among grants made to the conquistadors. Former colleagues at arms who knew the area insisted that López' Indians, a bare handful in number, were a poverty-stricken lot. Almost two decades after López had been assigned half of the pueblo of Tequixquiac, there were those in New Spain who still recalled the surprise among the general soldiery over the meagerness of the grant accorded the shipwright. Forty years after his entrance into New Spain, López still held half of Tequixquiac in encomienda; it still represented an inadequate income for him; and it never had been supplemented by any similar grant.

There is no indication that the worker-warrior from Seville ever saw the pueblo of Tequixquiac prior to its assignment to him. Like his eminent forebear in the conquest of Seville almost full three centuries earlier, López received land in the general neighborhood of the scene of his greatest military contribution. Whereas the warrior in Spain had received vineyards, olive groves, fig orchards, and rich acreage, Martín López' major grant in New Spain promised only years of penury and anxiety.[8]

Among the conquistadors, Martín López ranks as one of the earliest and most regular residents of Mexico City. Numerous factors help to account for his settled ways. By the mid-1520's Martín López was in his late thirties, older than the average conquistador and possibly more prone to forgo the rigors of further campaigning. Even in infant Mexico City he may have found an approximation of his Old World home. Furthermore, because of the slight reward he had received for his shipbuilding exploits during the conquest, López must have felt no urge to identify himself with Cortés' shipping projects on the Pacific, either at Zacatula or later at Tehuantepec. At any rate, the mid-twenties found him settling in Mexico City, destined to remain there almost constantly for half a century. Upon his return from Pánuco, López appeared before the municipal council (cabildo) with Juan Marquez, likewise a citizen of the young city, on April 15, 1524, with a petition to exchange their assigned building lots, indicating his intention to identify himself with the community.[9]

Mexico City really began as a full-blown community. Hernando

---

[8] López, 1528-1574, pp. 63, 72, 80-81, 106-107, 115, 122, 151, 184, Conway Coll. (Aberdeen); López, 1529-1550, pp. 122, 130, 138, 152, 166, Conway Coll. (LC).

[9] Actas de cabildo, I, 8. With the records of the municipality for the period before March 8, 1524, no longer extant, one is left to wonder exactly when the initial grants had been made.

Cortés, having determined the site and having supervised its earliest construction, provided it with a readymade government, as he transferred from Coyoacán the officials already established there. Late in 1522 the crown confirmed Cortés in the governorship of New Spain.

Governor Cortés made his greatest single peacetime contribution to the Hispanization of New Spain in the ordinances of March 20, 1524, which reflected much of the complexion of Spanish life in New Spain. Conquistadors receiving fewer than five hundred Indians were required to keep certain weapons on hand and be prepared for service in the infantry; those with more than five hundred Indians were bound to maintain a horse. Clearly established were the Spaniards' feudal-like right to the Indians and the concomitant responsibility to protect the new order. Reiterated was the Spaniard's obligation to promote the religious conversion of his Indian laborers. To achieve social and economic stability, a minimum residence of eight years was exacted of men receiving land and Indians; conquerors, if married, were to bring their wives to New Spain within eighteen months; if not married, they were to become so within the same period of time; and the same time period was likewise allowed them to build and occupy their houses.[10]

In strengthening the social fabric and moral tone of Spanish life in New Spain, Cortés was also serving the ends of the church. Father Juan Díaz and the Mercedarian Fray Bartolomé de Olmedo, the first Christian clergymen, had come with Cortés' original force. Through them the spiritual comforts of mass, communion, confession, and absolution had helped men facing enormous odds. Those same churchmen epitomized the continuing Spanish crusade as they preached Christian doctrine to the Indians, baptized native maidens given to conquistadors, and encouraged the replacement of pagan religious symbols by those of Christianity.

At the fall of Tenochtitlán the clergy in New Spain numbered

---

[10] J. F. Pacheco, F. Cárdenas, and others (eds.), *Colección de documentos inéditos relativos al descubrimiento, conquista y organización de las antiguas posesiones de América y Oceanía* (42 vols., Madrid, 1864-1884), XXVI, 135-48.

five. The Franciscan Pedro de Gante reached Vera Cruz in 1522 with two other Flemish Franciscans and soon established a Spanish-administered school for Indians at Texcoco. Mid-1524 found the Franciscans formally launching their religious labors, as Friar Benavente, destined to be remembered as Toribio Motolinía, and his cohorts entered the land.

Men of religious orders accompanied the Spaniards on their military expeditions, but they also established churches, founded monasteries, and initiated manifold educational and charitable works. One of the greatest forces in Spanish life, the clergy were the primary regulators of society, doing much, as they baptized, married, and buried Indian and Spaniard, to effect the reconciliation of two streams of culture. As they tempered the demands of the victor and gave hope to the vanquished, these religious workers, dignifying the process of miscegenation, served the ends of social justice in a society which otherwise was highly undemocratic and class conscious.

By early 1524 a clearer perception of the details of everyday life in Mexico City is possible. The cabildo met in weekly session to cope with problems facing the growing municipality. Solemnly the *alcalde mayor,* the *alcaldes ordinarios,* and the councilmen *(regidores),* occasionally honored and assisted by Governor Cortés himself, heard petitions, pondered problems, and formulated ordinances. Scarcely a cabildo session passed without the presentation of petitions by newcomers to the community: a man sought a piece of land on which to build a house; another petitioned for a garden plot; a third, desiring the fullest rights within the municipality, asked to be granted the status of citizen. Such matters kept the eighty-peso-per-year scribe of the cabildo quite busy. In like fashion, land transactions and other negotiations gave rise to increasing need for public scriveners.

Complaining residents cried out for relief from merchants who, making the most of a situation in which gold was more plentiful than goods, resorted to faulty weights and measures to increase profits. In city life, as well as among the conquistadors who had long groaned about the prices of nails and shoes for their mounts, the blacksmiths were an early object of complaint. The cabildo passed an ordinance which fixed the price of every single product of the blacksmith's shop. So, too, did butchers' shops draw private criticism and public regulation. Often heard in those days in the heart of Mexico City was the booming voice of town crier Francisco González, salaried at fifty gold pesos per year by the cabildo, as he informed the public of ordinances and other official news.

Maintenance of the city jail posed an early financial burden which was met in a unique way. Needing money for food for his prisoners, as well as a lamp and a religious statue in his gloomy quarters, the jailer was granted permission to ask alms of the public every Friday and Sunday.[11]

Defense of mushrooming Mexico City was endangered by the departure of many of the Spanish residents on private projects. Gold-hungry conquistadors took the Indians whose labor had been assigned to them off great distances to wash gold from the streambeds. To protect Mexico City, still too populated by the recent enemy for comfort, and to protect the abused Indians, such unauthorized departures from the city were henceforth prohibited and violators were subject to loss of their Indians.

On May 4, 1527, Martín López witnessed the signing of the pact which established the mining partnership of Juan Infante and Fray Ramón Bernal. Down to that moment about half of the companies notarized in Mexico City related to mining ventures. Many districts, but Oaxaca principally, were being combed for gold by the Spaniards with their Indian work gangs.[12]

Proof exists that this earliest wave of Spanish concern about mining in New Spain involved López personally. For an unknown period he had somewhat more than fifty Indian slaves working some twenty leagues to the southwest of Mexico City in the silver mines of Sultepec. Exactly how profitable this was to him is not established; but the removal by the audiencia of those Indians at the close of the decade represented, according to López, a loss of

---

[11] *Actas de cabildo*, I, 3-23 *passim*.

[12] *Ibid.*, 12, 137-38; Millares Carlo and Mantecón, *Indice y extractos*, I, no. 531 (also see pp. 378-81).

twenty thousand gold pesos. (The high valuation of the Indians is based on long-range expectation of income to be derived from their labor and is not an indication of their market value.) Lest an interested party's estimate be discounted heavily, support for the statement that heavy loss had been incurred by López was offered by Diego de Coría, the audiencia's inspector in the Sultepec area.

It is known also that 130 Indians jointly owned by López and fellow conquistador Alonso de Aguilar were in Olinalá in 1529, when López went with Nuño de Guzmán to New Galicia. Holder of the two encomiendas of Papaluta and Olinalá in Tlaxcala, Alonso de Aguilar was identified with mining over a considerable period of time, hence the inference that this little-known arrangement between him and López also might have concerned pursuit of mineral wealth.[13]

By the middle 1520's many of the artisan classes of Spain were represented in Mexico City: blacksmiths, carpenters, butchers, silversmiths, bladesmiths, pastry cooks, wax chandlers, surgeons, tailors, muleteers, apothecaries, glovemakers, saddlers, shoemakers, armorers, coopers, confectioners, stonecutters, tanners, hosiers, locksmiths, and numerous others. Conscientious muleteers, with their pack-laden animals, moved between port and interior as well as from town to town in the endless movement of goods and bullion which were the lifeblood of the economy of Spain's wealthiest colony. One richly revealing artisan career of this period is that of blacksmith Hernán Martín.

Like many of his fellow conquistadors who settled in New Spain, Hernán Martín believed his services had been poorly repaid. Lingering awhile in newly erected Mexico City, he was granted several pieces of property by the cabildo. On March 8, 1524, he received a piece of land on the north side of the road

---

[13] López, 1528-1574, pp. 154, 155, 169, Conway Coll. (Aberdeen); Francisco del Paso y Troncoso (comp.), *Epistolario de Nueva España, 1505-1818* (16 vols., Mexico City, 1939-1942), VIII, 119, 120; IX, 20; XIV, 94; XVI, 42; Díaz del Castillo, *Historia verdadera*, III, 225; Millares Carlo and Mantecón, I, no. 1188; II, no. 2610.

leading to Tacuba, about an arrowshot and a half beyond the hermitage erected by conquistador Juan Garrido in honor of the Spanish war dead. There the blacksmith already had erected a house. A week later, on March 15, 1524, he and his trade became the direct target of the earliest recorded piece of price-fixing legislation by Europeans in Mexico. The municipal government, in answer to the complaint that the blacksmiths were over-charging, fixed specific prices for the products of their labor. Obviously irked, Hernán Martín nonetheless remained in the infant metropolis for several more years. In October, 1527, and again in May, 1528, he petitioned the cabildo for land to supple-ment his holdings. In mid-1527 he figured as one of the spokes-men of the religious brotherhood *(cofradía)* of Santa Veracruz when it petitioned the cabildo of Mexico City for a site for a church and a hospital. A year and a half later the blacksmith, by then also steward of the Cofradía de la Santa Veracruz, was a party to certain documents in an effort to win a papal bull and indulgences for the recently founded brotherhood.

In late August, 1525, Martín and shipmaster Bartolomé Ro-dríguez formed an importing company, each investing three hundred pesos in the undertaking. With that capital the master was to transport from Spain to Santo Domingo, whence the blacksmith would import them into New Spain via the port of Medellín, the following supplies: 500 iron tools, principally hoes and bars; 6 *quintales* of iron; 2 *arrobas* of steel; 6 quintales of lead; and a good Negro slave. The remainder of the six hundred pesos was to be invested in good wine.

The next month, on September 14, 1525, the artisan-business-man was taking steps to complete the dissolution of a previous partnership. He then authorized a blacksmith resident in Mede-llín, García Martín, to collect from blacksmith Juan García of Villa Rica de la Vera Cruz the smithing tools which belonged to Hernán Martín by virtue of his earlier association with Juan García. In early 1527 he was entrusted with certain matters by blacksmith García Martín; and late in the same year Pedro

Hernández, a blacksmith in the Pacific port town of Zacatula, named Hernán Martín his agent in certain matters related to Mexico. Paralleling the introduction of the guild system, professional camaraderie of a high order, as indicated within this limited phase of Hernán Martín's occupational activities, existed in the early economic life of New Spain.[14]

Another proof of Martín López' identification with this developing economic life dates from August 27, 1527, when a merchant of the city was busy marketing certain wines, dry goods, and other merchandise which López had placed with him for sale.[15] With this transaction of mid-1527, but the first of several in which he dealt with merchants of the city, one suspects López did not hesitate to turn a peso now and then in the indirect sort of commercial activity to which an hidalgo might subscribe.

Able in some manner to avoid being drawn into the expeditions to Honduras which culminated in the one of late 1524 led by Cortés, Martín López was a witness in Mexico City to the mad struggle for power which took place in the governor's absence. Led by the rebellion in Honduras of his former captain Cristóbal de Olid to take the field in person once more, Cortés' lengthy absence between late 1524 and mid-1526 gave his personal enemies and certain ambitious royal officers opportunity to undermine his position. Insistent rumor of his death led many of Cortés' enemies to come into the open as never before. Throughout these shifting moments Martín López kept himself apart from the boiling political cauldron in Mexico City. His name is not on the long list of citizens pledging their loyalty on August 22, 1525.[16]

By late 1525 Martín López had taken up residence in the heart of Mexico City on a street which bore his name. A series of cabildo grants, dated November 28, 1525, permit a partial reconstruction of the neighborhood in which López then lived. The late shipbuilder's downtown property holdings, including the lot

14 *Actas de cabildo*, I, 4-6, 7, 12-13, 38, 74, 95, 133, 148, 149, 170; Millares Carlo and Mantecón, I, nos. 29, 66, 324, 335, 814, 1138, 1737-1738; Pacheco and others, XXVII, 159.
15 Millares Carlo and Mantecón, I, no. 739.
16 *Actas de cabildo*, I, 54-55.

on which his house stood, were on the west side of the present-day Calle Licenciado Verdad, extending northward from the point at which that street meets Moneda. (A subsequent sale of López' property facilitates the pinpointing of its location.) In late 1525, the street, which is now named for a precursor of the war of independence, was referred to in official municipal records as "la calle de Martín López." Precise reason for its being so named is not available, but probably it was because López had received the first grant on it. His property at the southern end of the street and nearest the plaza could easily have been the initial grant. Or was it so named because he was the most prominent resident upon it, or because so much of the land on it had initially belonged to him? On the latter score the records do suggest that at first López owned a number of building lots on the street. Indeed, on November 28, 1525, Román López, unrelated to the shipwright, was granted a building lot which cabildo records refer to as belonging to Martín López.[17]

Such conquistadors as Guillén de la Loa, Lucas de Montánchez, Gerónimo de Aguilar, Román López, Francisco de Solís, Pedro González Nájera, Francisco Rodríguez, and Francisco Mexia constituted the nearest neighbors of Martín López.[18] Guillén de la Loa, a notary employed by Francisco de Garay to take possession

[17] *Ibid.*, 62; José María Marroqui, *La Ciudad de México* (3 vols., Mexico City, 1900-1903), I, 7, 468, 472-73; Luis González Obregón, *Las Calles de México* (5th ed., 2 vols. in one, Mexico City, 1941), I, 4, 212.

[18] References to López' neighbors are in *Actas de cabildo*, I, 62; V, 150; Paso y Troncoso, I, 42, 127, 134-35; 142; VI, 4-5; IX, 10, 28, 31; XIII, 9, 39; XIV, 150, 154, 159; Pacheco and others, XIV, 37; XVI, 549, 553; XXVI, 234-36, 268-77, 360, 451, 464; XXVII, 16-17, 153-55, 157, 224, 441, 457, 476, 567; XXVIII, 101, 226, 317, 489, 494, 495; XXIX, 474; Millares Carlo and Mantecón, I, nos. 26, 28, 95, 108, 310, 313, 431, 478, 508, 510, 524, 526, 527, 536, 557, 587, 654, 673, 676, 686, 689, 714, 716, 726, 740, 773, 833, 843, 973, 988, 1052, 1181, 1221, 1226, 1227, 1229, 1240, 1273, 1325, 1328, 1353, 1381, 1440, 1554; II, nos. 1929, 2365-2367; Díaz del Castillo, *Historia verdadera*, I-III *passim*; Hernán Cortés, *Fernando Cortes—His Five Letters of Relation to the Emperor Charles V*, trans. and ed. by Francis Augustus MacNutt (2 vols., New York, 1908), I, 143-44; *Información de los méritos y servicios de Pedro González Nájera* (1526, 1528), Paso y Troncoso Coll., Leg. 94; Francisco González de Cossío, *El libro de las tasaciones de pueblos de la Nueva España—siglo XVI* (Mexico City, 1952), 315-16; López, 1528-1574, pp. 41-44, Conway Coll. (Aberdeen); Bermúdez Plata, *Catálogo de pasajeros*, I, 150.

of the Pánuco area, had led the first small group of Spaniards to be added to Cortés' force after the landing of 1519 in New Spain. Termed a "notable man" by Bernal Díaz, he served ashore during the siege of Tenochtitlán. In 1525 he lived directly opposite Martín López.

To one side of the notary lived Lucas de Montánchez, a little-known conquistador who traded in horses and pigs: witness his sale of two chestnut-colored packsaddle horses to muleteer Sancho Ramírez for 400 gold pesos. Less than two months later, on October 5, 1525, Montánchez sold Presbyter Martín Bachiller a chestnut saddle horse for 260 gold pesos and 48 pigs for an additional 144 pesos.

Flanking the notary's house on the other side was the residence of Gerónimo de Aguilar, male half of the famous pair of interpreters so important to Cortés in the conquest. This former aide eventually became one of the open enemies of Cortés, but in the midtwenties he may possibly have harbored only smoldering resentment like the shipwright across the street.

Contributing to the deterioration of relations between Cortés and Aguilar were these factors: Cortés' suppression of a royal grant of a perpetual post as councilman for Gerónimo de Aguilar in Mexico City, and Aguilar's legal battles (at least two) with Cortés, involving cows in one instance and remuneration for services in another. Aguilar looms large in the *pesquisa secreta* and *residencia* documents of 1529, clearly the foe of Cortés and the friend of Salazar and other royal officials. With the lot of Guillén de la Loa directly opposite the house of Martín López and the former's lot flanked by those of Montánchez and Aguilar, it is apparent that the shipwright's house was not at the street intersection, though he possibly owned the property between his residence and the corner.

Next door to prominent and politically active Aguilar was the property of Román López, a little-known and elusive figure. One thing he did not elude, however, was the responsibility for a 300-peso indebtedness which found him languishing momentarily in the Mexico City jail in late August, 1525.

Still on the opposite side of the street and off to the left from Martín López' house was the property of Francisco de Solís, next to that of Román López. Solís held several encomiendas, among them Tlacotepeque, near Chalco, and the pueblo of Aculman, remembered best for its monastery. He was, on occasion, both pro-Cortés and pro-López.

One of López' next-door neighbors on the west side of the street was Triana-born Pedro González Nájera, a conquistador who had served aboard ship during the famous siege of the Aztec capital. His many purchases, for which he contracted numerous debts in 1527, stamp him a man of fastidious tastes and possibly of some means as well. From a series of merchants and artisans he bought Spanish wines, silver candlesticks, and capes and cloaks of plush silk and velvet. His debts led to his being hounded by collectors, and possibly inspired his sale in mid-1528 of one hundred Indian slaves he then had searching for gold in Oaxaca.

On the north side of Martín López' residence was the home of Francisco Rodríguez. This carpenter from Seville was a worker on the thirteen brigantines and the shipping Cortés had ordered built at Zacatula. He later initiated two suits against Cortés for remuneration of labor expended on the pair of shipbuilding projects. In 1527 López sold a share in certain property he held to Rodríguez. For the sum of 300 gold pesos López not only surrendered the property but promised to use his Indians to complete certain portions of the structure. The size and nature of the building are unknown, but the price suggests it was not radically unlike other houses of Mexico City, for sale prices as of 1527 commonly ranged between 220 and 300 pesos. By the late twenties the ties of the common hometown in Spain, contiguous properties in Mexico City, and mutually bitter memories of their shipbuilding experiences had produced more than normal neighborly ties between the two men.

Residing in the second house to the north of the shipwright's residence, and the last of the eight men identifiable as neighbors of Martín López in 1525, was Francisco Mexia, a virtual unknown.

In this compact little group living within a stone's throw of the heart of Mexico City were men from various districts of Spain, some with and others without encomiendas, some the friends of Cortés and others his implacable enemies. The well-known and the unknown rubbed elbows; the politically active and the politically inert lived side by side. The residents on la calle de Martín López represented economic, social, and political diversity. They smacked of Spanish individualism, one of the richest cultural factors the mother country could bestow, through the medium of the conquistador class, upon its New World namesake.

The Cortés ruling of 1524 that single men marry and married men bring their wives to New Spain followed a tragic chapter in his own household. His spouse Catalina, who had made her way from Cuba to the land of his triumph in mid-1522, had died under mysterious circumstances. More than one wagging tongue suggested that the rich and powerful don Hernando, less than happy at her appearance, had been instrumental in her disappearance.

Another element of mystery attends the wife of the shipwright from Seville. Vague references to the first señora López suggest the conquistador brought her from Spain in 1526, a year which otherwise is a void in our knowledge of him. However interesting this information, it raises more questions than it supplies answers. Did Martín López make a trip to Seville in 1526? If so, did he go home to get married, or did he go for a wife who had remained behind the entire decade he had been in the Indies? If he had married prior to going abroad in 1516, he might merely have sent for her, although, of course, any ten-year expatriate Spaniard, and especially one who had participated in such a widely heralded adventure as the conquest of New Spain, well might have desired to saunter once more down the streets of Seville. Without knowledge of the date of his marriage and of his movements during 1526, we do know he had a Spanish wife with him in Mexico City early in 1527, in somewhat belated compliance with the ordinance of 1524.

Apparently Inés Ramírez, the first wife of Martín López, also came from Seville. The previously mentioned commercial arrangement in late summer of 1527 between López and a Mexico City merchant whereby the wines, dry goods, and other merchandise of the former were to be marketed raises the question: Did López return to New Spain with a cargo of Spanish merchandise as well as a Spanish wife? Remembering that he had originally entered the land in 1519 with an abundance of miscellaneous supplies, it is not unlikely that he repeated the performance, if, in fact, he made that trip of 1526. Apparently without issue, for no reference has been found to any child of Martín López by his first wife, Inés died sometime before 1529.[19]

Meanwhile, in this interval between the return of Cortés from Honduras and the worsening of that leader's position to the point where he felt it necessary to return to Spain, some of López' activities are recorded. On January 31, 1527, Martín López, having stood as surety for the passage expenses of Pedro de Fuentes, his nephew of the same name, and two servants, was called upon by Gaspar Pacheco for payment of the sum of forty-six gold pesos. The first of two documents executed that day closes with an excellent illustration of Martín López' signature—this, in fact, being the earliest extant one of which the author has knowledge.[20] His distinctive and easily read signature appears numerous times in the notarial records of the late 1520's.

Identified in the municipal records as a carpenter, López was granted on September 27, 1527, the garden plot *(huerta)* previously held by Juan Ruiz de Robles up to the time of his death. Located on the important street stretching between Mexico City and Tacuba, López' property was adjacent to that of Gonzalo Rodríguez de Ocano.[21] Like his continuing desire for a bigger and better encomienda, the habit of adding to his landholdings —building lots, gardening plots, ranching sites, and the like— developed into one of his insatiable appetites.

In 1528 and shortly thereafter, the citizen of Mexico City for

---

[19] López, 1528-1574, p. 72, Conway Coll. (Aberdeen); Millares Carlo and Mantecón, I, no. 1541.
[20] Millares Carlo and Mantecón, I, nos. 321, 323.
[21] *Actas de cabildo,* I, 148.

whom Calle Martín López was named stepped out of the easy-going pattern which had marked his life for some years. In turn he fought Cortés in the courts, accepted a post which took him away from Mexico City, and finally submitted to the pressure which took him off on one more campaign of military conquest. For López some explanation of changed behavior possibly lies in the disappointment and sorrow which attended his wife's death. But if peculiarly hectic activity came to López in the late 1520's, it was simply a matter of his finding a place in the general turmoil which plagued all New Spain.

## CHAPTER V

# THE SHAPE OF THINGS TO COME

ONE OF the significant early developments in New Spain was the sequence of events wherein Cortés the all-powerful became well-nigh powerless. Given the free-lance nature of the Cortés expedition to New Spain and the absolutism of the Spanish crown, a clash between Cortés and his king was inevitable. Add the phenomenal success of the conquistador captain general and the bitter enmity he had engendered in certain circles, and the certainty of a day of reckoning for him is plain.

The rift between Cortés and Governor Velázquez of Cuba had rapidly deepened. Cortés' initial flaunting of Velázquez' authority had irritated the Cuban official, and the subsequent successes of the bumptious man from Medellín served to fan his rage. To defeat his rebellious agent, Velázquez had sent the unsuccessful Narváez expedition of 1520, and he also had referred the entire matter to his friend Bishop Fonseca, long Spain's most powerful man in the management of New World affairs. Cortés had defeated native opposition in New Spain, and he had triumphed militarily over his Spanish foes as well; but the inexorable royal policy—especially as pursued by the distant, relentless, and powerful Fonseca—had no place in it for such a mighty upstart as Cortés.

In April, 1521, even as Cortés was readying his army and navy for the monumental siege of Tenochtitlán, his greatest military victory, the crown brought into the open the struggle don Hernando was destined to lose to royal authority. Cristóbal de Tapia was named to introduce royal rule into New Spain. The Christmas season of 1521 climaxed this first brush between Cortés and the royal will. In warding off this initial threat to his authority, as set forth earlier, Cortés demonstrated no small measure of the statesmanship which postponed considerably his day of final reckoning with the crown.

Fourteen months after the fall of Tenochtitlán and but a short time after Spanish receipt of word of Cristóbal de Tapia's failure to introduce royal authority into New Spain, the conquistador chieftain's position was defined for the first time by the crown. A royal cedula of October 15, 1522, named Cortés governor and captain general of New Spain, but emphasizing the fact that Cortés must share authority with royal agents was the simultaneous naming of four treasury officials for New Spain.[1]

In the months between his receipt of the cedula of late 1522 and his departure for Honduras in 1524, Cortés was at his peak as peacetime administrator. With the crown apparently satisfied and hence slow to send out the promised treasury officials (they arrived in New Spain in 1524), with opposition of the implacable Velázquez cut short by his death in June, 1524, and with the essential unity of his following still maintained, Cortés had what many students call his finest days. As governor, he enunciated sound military, religious, economic, and social policies. Many of the activities of Martín López grew out of Cortés' great

[1] Pacheco and others, *Colección de documentos inéditos*, XXVI, 65-70.

ordinances of March 20, 1524. These led López to assemble the
arms in his house to defend not only his household but the Spanish
community at large. The Cortés regulations also caused López to
bring his wife over from Spain. In his many endeavors to consolidate the Spanish position in New Spain and to advance the
Hispanization of the life of the land, Cortés contributed notably
to the creation of New World nationality.

However, this success was only momentary. When Cortés returned in mid-1526, a royal investigator, Luis Ponce de León,
appeared in Mexico City with authority to relieve Cortés of his
duties and conduct an investigation of his tenure of office. Hardly
was his coming known, before the investigator sickened and died
under circumstances that attached ugly rumors to the name of
Cortés. It was not difficult for a public that believed the conquistador leader had murdered his wife in 1522 to conclude
similar treatment had been accorded the royal official. But Ponce's
death merely transferred that official's authority as governor to one
Marcos de Aguilar. Old and feeble, Aguilar was no match for
Cortés; on his death in February, 1527, Aguilar bequeathed his
authority to royal treasurer Alonso de Estrada, one of the royal
appointees of October, 1522.

For a time ever-faithful Gonzalo de Sandoval had served with
Estrada as cogovernor of New Spain. But by late August, 1527,
Cortés' friend had been removed from office and royally appointed
Estrada had assumed sole responsibility for the government. As
a climax to this process which had gradually eased him from
authority, an unseemly quarrel between Cortés and Estrada led
the nonconquistador governor to banish the conquistador leader
from Mexico City. Then it was that Cortés, Sandoval, Andrés
de Tapia, and others began to collect the money, enlist the men,
and make all the other preparations necessary for a return to Spain.
Close crown management of affairs was evident in word that an
audiencia, an agency of government already established in the
Antilles, would soon assume control in New Spain. Expansion of
royal power and curtailment of Cortés' authority, accompanied by

changes and confusion dangerous to the stability of the colony, caused Cortés to resort to direct appeal to the Spanish throne.

For many men it was a season for decisions and action. Some prepared themselves for the trip to Spain with Cortés, ready to petition for offices and property, to battle for sizable shares of the fruits of victory. Others, now anti-Cortés, remained in New Spain, allied themselves with the agencies of royal control, and indeed even employed them as they engaged in legal battles with their onetime captain general.

Martín López turned to the courts as the year 1528 opened. On January 7 he executed a power of attorney on behalf of lawyer Francisco de Alva of Mexico City. The same day his friend and fellow brigantine-worker Andrés Núñez sought counsel from the same lawyer. The notarial records of the period indicate that attorney Francisco de Alva, one of a number in Mexico City of the profession which many of the conquistadors viewed as a scourge from which they hoped their New World home would be happily free, was a very busy man with his law practice.[2]

Although hostile to Cortés, many lesser conquistadors also resented the actions of the royal authorities. Thanks to royal grants, many mere settlers had fared as well as the original conquistadors, acquiring building sites, ranching and farming properties, public offices, and citizenship. Gaining little or nothing in their opposition to both Cortés and crown, some disgruntled veterans drifted on a sea of diverging loyalties. Often the shifting loyalties of the lesser men of New Spain—and certain of their activities—reflected the changing status of the duel between their former commander and the royal officials as well as the intensification of their personal disgruntlement.

The boldness of López was still with him when he spearheaded the court battles of the disgruntled brigantine builders. Through lawyer Francisco de Alva he filed a petition shortly before March 3, 1528, demanding payment from the captain general for services rendered during the conquest. In early March, as the court

---

[2] Millares Carlo and Mantecón, *Indice y extractos*, I, nos. 949-50.

requested presentation of proof by the plaintiff, López submitted a thirteen-item interrogatory which he asked leave to put to witnesses called on his behalf. Five points concerned the thirteen brigantines of 1520-1521, for the building of which the shipwright sought payment of 5,000 gold pesos. As a secondary subject, López introduced the building of the four brigantines, for which he asked payment of 2,000 gold pesos. The third and last theme was the caravel project, for which he asked recompense of 1,000 gold pesos.[3] For three shipbuilding episodes between 1519 and 1521 the short-term shipwright from Seville sought a total of 8,000 pesos in gold.

It should be borne in mind that López sought payment for exceptional services, not routine ones. Nowhere does he contest the share of the booty he had received.

The López interrogatory was put to each of ten men in Mexico City, and their testimony under oath was entered into the record. In order, the following witnesses testified: Diego Ramírez, Alvar López, Hernán Martín, Lázaro Guerrero, Melchor de Alabes, Alonso Cárdenas, Andrés Martínez, Juan Ramos de Lares, Antón de Rodas, and Hernando Alonso. All ten were conquistadors, veterans of the Tenochtitlán fighting; all were residents of Mexico City except Antón de Rodas, and he was there temporarily; all had known Martín López for at least seven years, and some from twelve to twenty-five years. None of the men was prominent in the life of Mexico City; five were artisans (three carpenters and two blacksmiths), and an equal number were relative unknowns. Although López did not stress the contribution of the thirteen brigantines, every witness called by him had personal knowledge of it. Nine of the ten witnesses clearly can be identified as coworkers of the shipwright on the thirteen-vessel project of 1520-1521. Six were sufficiently literate to sign their testimony.

On every point the testimony of the ten witnesses amounted to warm, often enthusiastic, support for López' position. Occasionally a witness' answer to a given question was such as to

[3] The record of this court action is in López, 1528-1574, pp. 4-56, Conway Coll. (Aberdeen).

amplify considerably the original assertion of the shipwright. (With deference to the fundamental justice of López' case and the truthfulness of the testimony, realism leads one to the cynical suggestion that the broader statements of some witnesses quite possibly were forerunners of their own suits against Cortés.) Eight of ten witnesses signified that Tenochtitlán could not have been taken without the thirteen-brigantine navy.

Notwithstanding the strength of such testimony, Martín López decided on March 10—by which date eight of the ten men had testified in Mexico City—to turn to six additional witnesses, all of whom were in the distant Pacific-coast town of Zacatula. Accordingly the plaintiff executed a document before a notary whereby he conferred his power of attorney upon Antón Sánchez and Cristóbal Hernández, residents of Zacatula.[4] In view of the distance and difficulties, Treasurer Estrada granted the plaintiff five months to get the desired testimony. On April 15, 1528, the testimony of the following men was recorded in Zacatula: Diego Hernández, Francisco Rodríguez, Rodrigo de Nájara, Clemente de Barcelona, Pedro Hernández, and Juan Gómez de Herrera.

The Zacatula witnesses bore marked resemblance to the men who had testified in Mexico City. Five of the six were able to sign their testimony, Clemente de Barcelona being the lone exception. All had helped Martín López on the thirteen brigantines, except perhaps Rodrigo de Nájara. Among the five identifiable artisans, two were carpenters, one was a blacksmith, one was a ship's calker, and one performed services whose nature is not known. They ranged in age from 29 to 37 years. Quite possibly all had been drawn to Zacatula by the shipbuilding under way there. All six Zacatula witnesses, veterans of the Tenochtitlán fighting, had known Martín López at least eight years, and some of them had been acquainted with the shipwright for twelve, fifteen, and even seventeen years. The substance of the Mexico City testimony was repeated in the words of the Zacatula witnesses.

Back in Mexico City, on May 20, 1528, attorney Francisco

---

[4] Millares Carlo and Mantecón, I, no. 1152.

de Alva presented the sealed Zacatula evidence to Governor Estrada and the court. Safely within the period allotted, that distant testimony had been taken, and López now had before the court an imposing file contributed by sixteen conquistadors. Late spring, 1528, must have found the shipwright confident of the outcome of his litigation.

To counter this array of support for the shipwright, the defense called only one witness, Francisco de Santa Cruz, a councilman of Mexico City. Testifying that many conquistadors who had received but thirty or forty pesos had contributed more to the victory, he belittled the amount of time and personal funds spent by the shipwright, and described the workers as men who had avoided arduous campaigning while they hammered ships together. He stated further that the shipwright had not stood watches in Texcoco while the brigantine-building was under way, and charged that the men of the brigantines repeatedly had pocketed loot during the siege of Tenochtitlán. (Santa Cruz' testimony disregarded truth to the extent that it provoked additional litigation, charges of perjury being leveled at him.)

Deciding in favor of the shipwright, the court ordered a board of referees appointed to determine the sum to which López was entitled. Six men were so designated: Martín Pérez, Francisco García, Francisco de Solís, Bernardino Vázquez de Tapia, Francisco de Terrazas, and Andrés de Tapia. Of that group the plaintiff had named the first two. There are reasons to believe the other four were designated in pairs by the court and the defendant, with Francisco de Terrazas and Andrés de Tapia the Cortés-named referees. Only the López-chosen representatives were well acquainted with shipbuilding.

The referees met repeatedly in an effort to agree upon the sum due the shipwright. Eventually four of the six were agreed. Unfortunately, the requirement that the decision of the referees be unanimous defeated the entire effort to conclude the issue.[5]

The refusal of the Cortés-designated referees to agree upon a

[5] López, 1529-1550, pp. 1-2, 4, 7-8, 9-10, 18-21, 56, Conway Coll. (LC); López, 1528-1574, pp. 60-61, 120, Conway Coll. (Aberdeen).

sum stemmed in part from Cortés' fear that the precedent-making
case would open a floodtide of litigation by lesser workmen if the
shipwright received an award. Cortés' absence in Spain since early
1528 and changes in administrative personnel helped prolong
the litigation.

Still other shipbuilders instituted court actions. One such
artisan-litigant was Diego Hernández, the bragging sawyer identified with all three of the shipbuilding projects. With the fall of
Tenochtitlán his sawing did not cease, because he then hurried
down to the coast to aid for a couple of months in the building of
a fortress at Villa Rica de la Vera Cruz. Once again back in the
Valley of Mexico, he was called upon to make doors and casement
windows for the residence of Hernando Cortés. Plying his trade
in Mexico City, Hernández drifted into the growing anti-Cortés
camp and finally joined the throng suing the captain general.

Without benefit of counsel, the destitute sawyer appeared
before the audiencia on October 26, 1529. Stressing his labors
upon seventeen brigantines, the unsuccessful catapult built during
the siege of Tenochtitlán, and an unknown number of artillery
carriages, as well as the forementioned doors and window case-
ments, Hernández insisted that he, not even the recipient of a
small encomienda, had never been paid for his services. (Four
centuries later one Mexican student of the conquest suggested
the erection of a statue in commemoration of Diego Hernández'
contributions to the introduction of European culture into the
New World.[6]) Extreme poverty led him to ask the court to
designate Francisco Morzillo, lawyer for the poor, as his counsel.
The audiencia complied with the request, and the sawyer proceeded to execute a power of attorney in favor of Morzillo. The
plaintiff demanded 1,000 pesos for work on the ships and a like
sum as his part of the booty retained by Cortés. (Seeking at least
200 pesos for his work on the four brigantines in Tenochtitlán
and 500 pesos for five months labor on the thirteen brigantines,

    [6] Francisco Fernández del Castillo, "Algunos documentos del Archivo del
Marquesado del Valle (Hospital de Jesús)," Boletín de la Sociedad Mexicana de
Geografía y Estadística, XLIII (1931), 24.

the sawyer also sought 200 pesos for his postconquest work on a fortress at Villa Rica de la Vera Cruz.) With Cortés absent from New Spain, the defense devolved upon attorney Altamirano.[7]

Lawyer Delgadillo, the member of the audiencia serving as judge in this instance, decided, on February 12, 1530, in favor of Diego Hernández. He ordered Cortés to pay Hernández four hundred pesos in gold and also the costs of the case.

An appeal by the defense consumed six months but was denied, and Delgadillo on August 1, 1530, ordered approximately eighty slaves owned by Cortés to public sale. On August 8, the court ordered Cortés to pay the plaintiff not only the four hundred pesos for unrewarded services but also twenty-eight more to cover his trial expenses.

Like the case of Diego Hernández, those initiated by carpenters Francisco Rodríguez and Andrés Núñez against Cortés are intimately related to the Martín López litigation. In neither the Rodríguez nor the Núñez case is the available record so full as that for Diego Hernández. Francisco Rodríguez, who had been a López worker on the last of the three shipbuilding projects, had continued such work for Cortés in the captain general's earliest Pacific Ocean shipbuilding efforts, those at Zacatula. For his work on the thirteen brigantines Rodríguez sought payment of 2,000 pesos from Cortés, and for similar services at Zacatula he asked, in a separate court action, an equal sum. The outcome of the suits is unknown. Another artisan-conquistador with a suit pending against Cortés at the time of the residencia of the captain general was blacksmith Hernán Martín.[8]

The connection between these artisans' cases against Cortés and that of López is evident when it is recalled that López called Diego Hernández, Hernán Martín, and Francisco Rodríguez to support his case. Meanwhile, Hernández in his suit also utilized testimony

---

[7] The record of this action is in Docs. Various Suits, 67-89, 92-133, Conway Coll. (Cambridge). See also, Eduardo Sánchez-Arjona, "Relación de las personas que pasaron a esta Nueva España, y se hallaron en el descubrimiento, toma e conquista della," *Revista de Archivos, Bibliotecas y Museos*, ser. 3, XXXVI (1917), 423-24.

[8] Pacheco and others, XXVII, 157, 159. Both actions probably occurred in 1529.

from Rodríguez. Andrés Núñez and Martín López apparently
had emerged close friends from the Tenochtitlán fighting. Each
held half of the village of Tequixquiac in encomienda. Perhaps
it was there, about 55 kilometers due north of Mexico City, that
López and Núñez became ranching partners. These men must
have planned a one-two blow against Cortés, but unlike that of
López, the course and outcome of the Núñez court battle with
Cortés cannot be traced. Patent, however, is the truth of Gonzalo
Rodríguez de Ocano's statement that "now they [the Spanish
shipbuilders] are all suing don Hernando for their work."[9]

Always a man of parts, López' total energy could not be consumed by his legal assault upon Cortés. On February 17, 1528,
Hernando de Cantillana, a shoemaker-merchant with whom López
had had prior business dealings, sold the shipwright four dozen
goatskins, four cowhides for sole leather, and two Spanish hides.
For those shoemaker's supplies a total of 175 gold pesos was paid,
but we have no indication that López made direct use of these
items, although they must have been part of either a business
enterprise or a commercial venture.[10]

Every time the cabildo took further concrete steps to implement
the plan established for the city, the conquistadors would seek
and receive additional land grants. One such occasion, on which
a block of land was subdivided into garden plots and granted to a
considerable number of the citizens of the city, was May 20, 1528.
That day López received a plot of land which lay along the road
between Chapultepec and Tacubaya. Five months later, on October 16, 1528, López asked the cabildo to grant him a small piece
of ground adjacent to the land previously given him in the
Tacubaya area.[11] Apparently López had checked the pattern of
grants immediately adjacent to his and had discovered a piece
of unassigned land.

The location of López' gardening plots (and there is reason

---

[9] López, 1529-1550, p. 111, Conway Coll. (LC).
[10] Millares Carlo and Mantecón, I, no. 1095.
[11] *Actas de cabildo*, I, 170, 184. The plan for early Mexico City, often referred
to in cabildo records as *la traza*, has never been found.

to believe he received even more such land) is interesting. The grant of September, 1527, lay between Tacuba and Mexico City, and the grant of May, 1528, along with the supplementary one of October of that year, lay between Chapultepec and Tacubaya. Martín López thus was party to a general westward movement evident in the overall pattern of land grants in the environs of Mexico City. However, there is nothing particularly original about such Spanish action, for the natives previously had exhibited a marked preference for the western shore of Lake Texcoco, and in this westward movement the conquerors were ratifying native choices made centuries earlier.

Meanwhile, López was faced with settling the estate of his deceased first wife. (The cause of her death is unknown, but the rigors of travel, living in the New World, and childbirth did claim many Spanish women of the period.) With the death of Inés Ramírez, widower López authorized four residents of Seville to receive certain of her properties to which he had fallen heir. To facilitate the labors of his agents in Spain, the shipwright entrusted, on September 19, 1528, a bar of gold worth 79 pesos 2 *tomines* to ship captain Cristóbal Sánchez of Triana, who was en route to Seville.[12]

12 Millares Carlo and Mantecón, I, nos. 1541, 1544.

# CHAPTER VI

# SERVANT OF THE FIRST PRESIDENT

THE DAWNING of 1529 in New Spain saw the emergence of Nuño de Guzmán. The crown had decided to introduce an audiencia into that land. The four judges (*oidores*) who composed it were directed by President Nuño de Guzmán, who had been in conflict with Cortés ever since his appearance in 1527 on the coast of New Spain as governor of Pánuco. Late December, 1528, with Cortés in the mother country, the president and oidores were in Mexico City, ready to start New Spain off on a different administrative foot.

As Nuño de Guzmán entered upon his duties January 1, 1529, New Spain was torn by highly explosive factionalism. The rash of litigation by the conquistadors against Cortés was but symptomatic of the times. Martín López was one of the disgruntled litigants whose loyalty shifted from Cortés to Nuño de Guzmán. Like many others, he elected to cooperate with the man in whose hands his future rested. It was not a question of deteriorating standards of values as men turned from Cortés to Guzmán; nor was it a question of which was the better leader, the stronger personality, the man of nobler purpose. It was simply a facing of the fact that Cortés symbolized the past, whereas Guzmán represented the future.

Until the arrival of the first audiencia in Mexico City, Martín López had not identified himself with the political life of New Spain. Considering both his Spanish background and his part in the conquest, it might be thought surprising that he did not aspire to a position in Mexico City. Like so many other things, the cabildo experienced considerable change, in personnel and otherwise, during the 1520's. At times it had elements of real democracy in its elections and composition, and reflected the heterogeneity of outlook in the young city. There were moments when Cortés controlled the municipality. In time, royal appointees challenged conquistador control by introducing the concept of life terms for some councilmen. Never, in all this confusion, did López participate directly in politics, although a number of equally individualistic conquistadors like Antonio de Carvajal, Bernardino Vázquez de Tapia, and Gonzalo Mexia did enjoy political prominence. Indeed, former conquistadors usually had a majority in the cabildo, and they rushed to fill lesser offices as well.

Although he apparently came forward for his share every time the municipal authorities distributed building lots and gardening plots, Martín López knew no other tie with affairs of government prior to the coming of the first audiencia. Apparently he sought no council seat, nor was he considered for the post of alcalde ordinario. Because he was never a councilman, López was ineligible for such posts as procurator and administrator of the property of deceased persons, since they were invariably subsidiary responsibilities of councilmen. Virtually all the posts not filled by members of the cabildo, as porter and town crier, were beneath a person of his station.

With the appearance of the first audiencia, López decided to seek office. The audiencia needed a man to go to Tehuantepec to replace and then conduct the residencia of Francisco Maldonado, a Cortés appointee supervising a shipbuilding project there. Shipbuilder López was an obvious choice for such an assignment, and in the spring of 1529 he was so designated.

Cortés had sent his loyal aide Francisco Maldonado to Tehuantepec in 1526 to administer the region in which his Pacific shipbuilding endeavor centered. In 1529 the audiencia not only was intent upon investigating and replacing such Cortés-named personnel, but, armed with a royal ruling limiting the use of Indians as porters, it was also in a position to paralyze this favorite project of Cortés which conceivably might outshine the conquest of New Spain as a personal triumph. Knowingly and willingly López became the monkey wrench thrown into the Tehuantepec plans of Cortés by the first audiencia.

With characteristic detail, which in this case concerned the subjects of tribute, shipping, port facilities, and religion, López' instructions, cast in three documents, one undated and the others dated April 27 and May 26, 1529, made it obvious the one-year appointee was to be a busy man in Tehuantepec.[1]

During the summer of 1529 two small clusters of Spanish horsemen traversed the 140 leagues of mountains, valleys, and plateaus between the city of Mexico and the pueblo of Tehuantepec. Heading southeastward from the seat of the audiencia late in June went a handful of newly appointed officials. About the figure of tall, 40-year-old Martín López—off to his jurisdiction as alcalde mayor—was assembled a company destined to serve as tax collectors, constables, and the like. Optimism and high humor surely keynoted the exchanges of men headed for salaried respon-

[1] Francisco Maldonado contra Martín López, 1533-1539, III, 87-96, Conway Collection (Cambridge University); the document is reproduced in Guillermo Porras Muñoz, "Martín López, carpintero de ribera," Instituto Gonzalo Fernández de Oviedo, *Estudios Cortesianos—recopilados con motivo del IV centenario de la muerte de Hernán Cortés (1547-1947)* (Madrid, 1948), 319-23. A published summation of López' activities in Tehuantepec is in C. Harvey Gardiner, "Tempest in Tehuantepec, 1529: Local Events in Imperial Perspective," *Hispanic American Historical Review*, XXXV (1955), 1-13.

sibilities and honors. In September the second lot of horsemen plodded toward Mexico City, a grim, uncommunicative group. Francisco Maldonado, the dominant figure, had reason to be sullen, dejected, and angry—as might any discredited former office-holder approaching prison. The guards attending him looked for their orders to muleteer Cristóbal de Castromocho, momentarily serving as constable. Between the coming of López and the departure of Maldonado, the tiny and unattractive frontier pueblo of Tehuantepec played host to a bitter incident in the struggle between Hernando Cortés and Nuño de Guzmán.

Initially a Narváez man, Maldonado had speedily shifted to Cortés. Appointed by the captain general to further a regional conquest as well as to superintend the important shipbuilding project on the isthmus, he led the contingent assigned him in war and peace. Centering his political administration in the pueblo of Tehuantepec and his fleet project at nearby Santiago on the coast, Maldonado established two small Spanish communities. Followers who originally bore arms with expectation of booty turned to smithing and carpentering and calking at fixed wages, Spanish workmen receiving a minimum of ten pesos monthly.[2] Despite recurring problems related to manpower and materials, the Cortés appointee pressed forward with his assignment. By the time López appeared in the isthmus, Maldonado had spent almost three full years there.

López, meanwhile, had executed the half circle from loyal supporter to implacable enemy of Cortés. Armed with commission and instructions for his three-phase authority as judge of the residencia, alcalde mayor, and captain of the province of Te-huantepec, he headed for his jurisdiction in mid-1529 intent upon consolidating the authority of the audiencia, weakening the position of Cortés, and gaining revenge upon his onetime commander. The questions and suspicions which greeted López on his arrival in Maldonado's seat of power were answered quickly on July 5, when town crier Bartolomé Destepa walked about the plaza pro-

---

[2] Hospital de Jesús, 300/107 (Archivo General de la Nación, Mexico City).

claiming the authority of the new alcalde mayor and the residencia of his predecessor.[3] The singsong routine of Destepa's stentorian announcement was prelude to seventy-five action-packed days.

Long before the prescribed residencia proceedings dictated his appearance before the new alcalde mayor, Francisco Maldonado tested the mettle of his successor. Between July 6 (López' second day in office) and July 19 (two days prior to the final formulation of the interrogatory for the pesquisa secreta) the old official and the new tangled on three occasions.

On the first occasion, Maldonado demanded to be allowed to collect tributes for the previous nine months, during which he had been in Mexico City. López' rapid rejection of his request was rooted in certain of his instructions. The audiencia had directed López to compile and forward to his superiors in Mexico City a list of the tributes to be collected in the region, and to see to it that no further tribute payments, in any form, were made to Cortés or his agent Maldonado. The new order categorically denied the old regime the lifeblood of power the tribute represented.

One week later, on July 14, Maldonado reappeared before López. Citing delays, the cost of Spanish labor, the continuing need for Indian workers, and the unfinished state of the vessels, Maldonado requested continued use of Indians of the villages of Tehuantepec, Xalapa, Guazontlán, and Ystatepeque (Istrectepeque?) as necessary to the completion of the ships.

Whereas he previously had presented a simple, direct request to López, Maldonado now employed a more complex and indirect technique. With his report on the necessity for Indian labor, he insisted that López must bear limited financial responsibility for the ships' materials on the mountain slopes; but he was silent regarding the total value of the shipping.

Even as he stopped Maldonado's further use of Indian labor, López tantalized his predecessor by proclaiming Maldonado's right to continue the project with the Spanish laborers he had on hand. López announced a 200-*castellano* fine would be levied

[3] *Ibid.*

against any Spanish artisan who refused to work for Maldonado on the ships. (One suspects this maneuver by López was legal subterfuge: openly it suggests his cooperation with Maldonado and continues Maldonado's responsibility for the ships; meanwhile, López cagily escapes responsibility for the sabotage effort to which he is dedicated.) Any decision regarding shipping found López exercising considerable discretion, because his instructions simply charged him with surveying existing and potential port facilities, determining what ships were on hand, advising the audiencia of the steps required to complete any unfinished shipping, and determining at whose expense previous ship construction had been pursued. The second visit of Maldonado to the new alcalde mayor's office supplied answers for more than one of those questions.

From his own experience as a successful shipbuilder in New Spain, Martín López knew that Indian labor was indispensable. Thanks to the Indians, the Tehuantepec project had been self-liquidating, with free Indian labor and Indian tribute payments covering the costs posed by Spanish labor and materials. The termination of Maldonado's right to collect tribute and freely use Indian labor constituted fatal blows to Cortés' shipbuilding prospects on the isthmus. López realized that his second rebuff of Maldonado wrote "finis" rather than "delay" across the shipping project. Subtly and with certainty the audiencia and it chosen agent, by paralyzing the shipping program, were administering a slap to Cortés and his Pacific prospects.

With the stakes high (no one knows what promises Cortés made to him) the persistent Maldonado came before López a third time, on July 19. He closed an extended and repetitious plea for permission to use Indian labor with testy insistence that López either make that concession or assume full responsibility for the investment the unfinished fleet represented, a sum in excess of 20,000 gold pesos. Maldonado was in no position to force López' acceptance of his "either-or" proposition, and the new alcalde mayor ended the verbal sparring by pointing out that his instructions gave him no authority to take possession of the ships.[4]

Even as this series of exchanges occurred, the new alcalde mayor was proceeding with the residencia of his predecessor. By July 21 a thirty-eight-item interrogatory clearly reflecting López' instructions was readied for the pesquisa secreta. Between that date and August 9 eight witnesses presented testimony. López carefully compiled evidence from men closely identified with Maldonado in Tehuantepec. Four of the eight witnesses, literate Diego García de Colio, cardplaying Francisco del Barco, disgruntled Pedro Asencio, and majordomo Francisco de Paz, had served as constables under Maldonado. Onetime servant Luys de la Cueva had been elevated to scribe. Illiterate García Martín, a blacksmith who had worked on the Tehuantepec ships some two years, was one of Maldonado's cardplaying cronies, having lost a gray saddle mare to the Cortés appointee on one occasion. Portuguese ropemaker Blas Hernández, initially a soldier with Maldonado in the conquest of Tehuantepec province and subsequently an employee in the shipyard at Santiago, was another who testified during the inquiry. The last witness, formerly a soldier under Maldonado and more recently that man's personal servant, was Pedro Martín, destined shortly to be a central figure in López' proceedings against Maldonado.[5]

With the verification of the testimony completed by August 25, López speedily formulated thirteen charges and ordered that Maldonado be seized and held in custody. Briefly, the charges against Maldonado were that he had gambled, had failed to obtain royal authority in a number of appointments, had failed to account for royal revenues, had collected excessive taxes, and had failed in religious instruction of the natives, roadbuilding, and a number of other technicalities. Between the lines one senses that the judge of the residencia was hard put to establish a case against Maldonado.

[4] *Ibid.*

[5] The record of this case is in Maldonado contra López, I, 12-16, 43-53, 117, 119; II, 34-37, 39, 47-48, 51-66; III, 18-77, 109-19; IV, 8-11, Conway Coll. (Cambridge).

Notified on August 26 of the charges against him, Maldonado appeared before López and made a stout defense of his official behavior, indicating that frontier conditions made it impossible to carry out minutely the ideas embodied in royal regulations.

In August and September, 1529, the simmering political conflict came to a boil. At the request of Constable Luys de la Cueva, a former servant of Maldonado who had been won to López' side, the new alcalde mayor subjected vagrant Spaniards in his jurisdiction who did not depart from the province within three days to a fine of 100 gold pesos and 100 lashes. On August 12 López fined a servant of Maldonado, 22-year-old Pedro Destrada, 25 gold pesos on the twin charges of employing ten Indians as porters without a license and failing to pay them for their labor. For maladministration of their offices, López banished constables Diego de Mena and Diego de las Casas from the province, with the added threat that their return would subject them to loss of all property and a death penalty. The appointee of the first audiencia was ridding his jurisdiction of both Maldonado and his subordinates.

On September 15 the struggle between López and the Maldonado faction reached a new and critical stage. Seized as a vagrant, Pedro Martín, a longtime follower and servant of Francisco Maldonado, was on trial before López. With weapons at his side and with noisy insistence that he be allowed to speak in behalf of his servant, Maldonado interrupted the judicial proceedings and caused minor uproar in the courtroom. During the commotion the former official mouthed a succession of robust epithets impugning the character of Martín López and the quality of royal justice. López immediately had six witnesses testify regarding the irregular courtroom behavior of Maldonado, and in less than twenty-four hours the agent of Cortés was ordered sent as a prisoner to the audiencia in Mexico City.

López immediately initiated an inventory of his predecessor's property. Accompanied by notary, constable, and witnesses, the alcalde mayor went to Maldonado's quarters in Tehuantepec and inventoried the personal property found in a succession of boxes and trunks. Discovering several locked containers, López sent to his prisoner for the necessary keys. When Maldonado, ill disposed to cooperate with his persecutor, refused to yield the keys in order to facilitate López' sequestration of his property, the latter ordered the locks broken. Item by item the personal property of Maldonado was listed—account books, saddle horses, a library of sixteen volumes, military equipment ranging from bullet molds to a coat of mail, golden necklaces and other jewelry, a fine wardrobe which included white stockings and velvet shippers and doublets of brown damask, white linen, and blue velvet, and a black plush silk coat, numerous tools such as knives, handsaws, axes, and hammers, watchglasses, mariners' compasses, a brandnew saddle, and a white Berber slave named Catalina. Maldonado was undoubtedly one of the wealthiest Spaniards between Mexico City and Panama, and López presumably wished to relieve himself of responsibility for his prisoner's property. Accordingly he designated Francisco de Paz, Maldonado's majordomo, as depositary.

López also provided for a second inventory of Maldonado's property in the nearby port of Santiago. On September 27 the alcalde mayor named Francisco Regodón as the notary before whom the Santiago inventory was to be recorded. The next day the property at the shipyard was listed, with considerable attention to detail. The notary recorded the name and stage of construction of each ship. Into the inventory went every pile of ships' timbers, commonly with the number and special names of the finished pieces as well as information concerning the kinds of wood from which they were made. The quantity and variety of tools inventoried probably represented one of the largest collections then in the New World: axes, adzes, chisels, hoes, spades, saws, chains, grindstones, forges, bellows, anvils, nail and spike molds, hammers, files, punches, awls, pliers, and brace drills. Again López named Francisco de Paz depositary of the sequestrated property. Meanwhile, Constable Cristóbal de Castromocho was escorting prisoner Maldonado to Mexico City.

Viewed in isolation, the bitter López-Maldonado clash is a tempest in a teapot, tendentious quibbling attending a minor administrative change; but viewed in relation to major forces then present in Spanish life in New Spain, the isthmian episode is a key to the times. With successive waves of royal cedulas and royal officials appropriating one phase after another of Cortés' authority, finally, as the first audiencia came out from Spain, Cortés voyaged homeward. As he went to Spain and the fountain-head of authority to fight his case, Cortés left numerous representatives behind to skirmish against royal officials in New Spain in defense of his interests. The chief seat of authority in New Spain, infant Mexico City, seethed with ever-increasing factionalism. The Maldonado-López incident in a remote frontier pueblo reveals how completely and intensely the Cortés-Guzmán struggle permeated all New Spain.

In this controversy additional facets of the personality of Martín López are revealed. Failing to get the reward he felt he deserved from Cortés, the satisfaction he might have known in moments of recollection yielded to a feeling of burning resentment and desire for revenge. Shifting to the anti-Cortés camp, he was ready and willing to serve the purposes of the first audiencia when it arrived in New Spain. The normal conquistador characteristic of self-serving ambition assumed, in López' activities in Tehuantepec, an abnormal pattern of bitter vindictiveness and gross unfairness.

There can be no doubting the fact that his handling of Maldonado demanded great personal courage, despite the fact royal authority was on López' side. (It must be remembered that one earlier royal official in New Spain who faced hostile unanimity had been blinded, another had been forced to withdraw, and a third had died under questionable circumstances.) Bearding a lion in his den, López not only encountered the full fury of an able fighter, he also fell heir to the hostility of almost the entire population of Tehuantepec. Many of the hangers-on, who were so numerous as to constitute a veritable retinue for Cortés' agent, were about to lose their easy way of life. Likewise, many honest

Spanish workmen, accustomed to wages from the purse of Maldonado, were now unemployed. López was the object of their common hatred as he sent Maldonado north as a prisoner. Some practices resorted to by López—the temporary shackling of the prisoner, the sequestration of his property against the possibility of fines and penalties emerging from his brush with the audiencia, the use of an unusual number of guards as escort, starting the trip between Tehuantepec and Antequera at night, and his appeal to Alcalde Mayor Peláez de Berrio of Antequera for assistance in getting the prisoner to Mexico City—are easily understood when one realizes that as López built his case against Maldonado, he had to live and operate in a community in which there was scarcely a single Spaniard he could call his friend.

His conduct of the residencia of Maldonado stressed other sides of his personality. In the aggregate the documents resulting from his experience as alcalde mayor suggest that López was a stickler for legal form, repeatedly replying to Maldonado, for example, in such manner as to indicate his awareness of and rigid adherence to his instructions. Out to discredit as well as to remove Maldonado, López could and did serve selfish personal interest in Tehuantepec as he complied with instructions intended to further selfish royal interests. Some of his replies reflect his knowledge of his relationship, as an alcalde mayor, to the audiencia and the crown. Such precision in the conduct of his office might easily have been an extension of the precise nature which had made possible a prefabricated navy on an earlier occasion. López' mind seemingly ran to logical arrangement and mastery of detail, without neglect of the final, large objectives to be served. Failing to realize one of his personal, large objectives under Cortés—generous reward for services during the conquest—López pursued the same end in the service of the audiencia; and the more completely he wrecked Cortés' prospects in Tehuantepec, the more he hoped to brighten his deferred chance at affluence.

In a period in which verbosity marks many legal papers, the statements of López during the residencia are masterpieces of brevity and directness. Either Alcalde Mayor Martín López had a most unusual scrivener in his employ, or the onetime shipwright was himself of pungently purposeful address, avoiding no issues and wasting no words.

The view of the personality of Francisco Maldonado which emerges is likewise revealing. Realistic and mercenary, he had shifted from the side of Narváez to that of Cortés. Loyal and ambitious, too, he spent years in Tehuantepec as Cortés' appointee —fighting natives, building ships, establishing Spanish authority. Persistent and determined, Maldonado reappeared before his successor even though he already had been rebuffed repeatedly. A man with numerous horses, a veritable arsenal, and a wardrobe such as would meet the needs of a sophisticated citizen of Seville, Maldonado carried to the frontier some sixteen printed volumes, possibly the largest private lay library then in that part of the New World. His resentment and his injured pride and desire for revenge subsequently inspired years of litigation with Martín López concerning the events of mid-1529 in Tehuantepec.

Studiously avoiding conduct which might someday lead to the leveling of similar charges against him, López could and did insist, in later life, that as alcalde mayor he had always treated the Indians well. On one occasion it seems he refused to accept three costly pieces of jewelry which certain Indian leaders offered him. The record of López' fair handling of Indian questions and his honest relations with them does not fall from his lips alone. Strange to say, all this occurred while López was serving audiencia and crown without salary.

The former shipwright's assertion that he served as alcalde mayor in Tehuantepec without salary or other remuneration—a fantastic thought—is not supported by his commission, for it assigned to him the rights and salaries pertaining to his posts. However, his failure to complete his one-year term of office might explain, in part, his failure to receive his salary. No available record suggests López ever tried to collect the unpaid sum. Did he feel that the opportunity to even a score with Cortés was sufficient recompense in itself? Extant records do little to resolve this subjective issue.

Although appointed for one year, López returned to Mexico City in the autumn of 1529, having served less than half his assigned term. Perhaps he accomplished his ends in Tehuantepec in scant six months and saw no reason to remain there any longer. Perhaps he was called to Mexico City by the threat of Maldonado-inspired litigation. The arrest and lodging of charges against Francisco de Santa Cruz, sole witness for Cortés in his court battle of 1528 against López, sufficiently reactivated López' fight for remuneration of his services during the conquest that he might have found it necessary, as well as desirable, to return to the principal seat of authority. Any and all of these reasons could explain the abbreviated term López served as alcalde mayor.

Antiaudiencia estimates of his service in Tehuantepec are not available beyond Majordomo Francisco de Terrazas' mention, in a document replete with detail concerning many men: "to Tehuantepec went Martín López the shipwright."[6] The fractional part of a sentence so dedicated to López seemed to carry with it the connotation—"what more need be said about this archenemy of yours?" On August 27 Bishop-designate Zumárraga addressed to his monarch a lengthy appraisal of the state of affairs in New Spain. Citing specific instances of the manner in which the audiencia had turned to acknowledged enemies of Cortés, the churchman included López obliquely by declaring that the audiencia had given jurisdiction in Tehuantepec to a man who had followed the career of shipwright in New Spain.[7]

The final appraisal of the officeholder, so commonly provided in New Spain by the records of a *visita* or a residencia, is made difficult in the case of Alcalde Mayor Martín López by the absence of any such documents.

Meanwhile, López had scarcely set out for Tehuantepec in mid-1529 when an event occurred which related him to still another significant area of Spanish endeavor in New Spain. The

---

6 Paso y Troncoso, *Epistolario de Nueva España*, I, 142.
7 Pacheco and others, *Colección de documentos inéditos*, XIII, 130.

announcement of the cabildo ordinance of Wednesday, June 16, 1529, made necessary the registering of livestock brands within twenty days.[8]

The ranching interests of Martín López, little known though occasionally hinted at in the record, began sometime in the 1520's. Given the Spaniard's twin affections for riding rather than walking and eating meat in preference to most other foods, it had been natural for the livestock industry to enter New Spain with the earliest conquistadors. First had come the horses and pigs, the former to carry the captains, the latter to supplement the food supply. More difficult to identify in time is the appearance of the first sheep and cattle, though conquistador Gregorio de Villalobos claims to have introduced, from Española within several years of the fall of Tenochtitlán, the first yearling calves into the land.[9] Given the climatic and topographical nature of New Spain and the Spanish ranching tradition which had already seen various types of animals transported from the mother country to the Caribbean islands, it was not long before some of the conquistadors employed acreage and Indians in this deep-rooted Spanish occupation.

Regulation of the prices and other aspects of the meat-supply system in Mexico City can be traced as far back as March 15, 1524. At a moment for which we have but scant information concerning the production and consumption of meat products, certain information on prices is invaluable. The four-pound unit *(arrelde)* of pork which cost 6 *reales* on March 15, 1524, fell to 1½ reales by October 10, 1525, and slumped further by March 15, 1526, to 20 *maravedis,* a price which held firm two years later. This rapid decline in the value of pork, a persistently popular item in the colonial diet, mirrors indirectly the great increase in hog raising in New Spain. That popularity is attested by the fact that the earliest references to the slaughterhouses and meat markets of Mexico City concern pork and pork alone. Likewise, herds of pigs,

[8] *Actas de cabildo,* II, 3.
[9] Información de los méritos y servicios de Gregorio de Villalobos (1554), Paso y Troncoso Coll., Leg. 97.

destined to feed hungry gold-hunting work gangs, figure promin-
ently in the mining-supply contracts of the mid-1520's.

With the middle twenties the beef and mutton supply also had
drawn the attention of municipal authorities. In the earliest years
these two ranch products commanded the same price, which
generally was at least five times greater than the price of pork.
The four-pound unit of beef or mutton which cost 3½ reales on
March 25, 1526, rose to 5 reales on May 7, 1527, and then declined
to 2½ reales on March 29, 1528. Though there was fluctuation of
beef and mutton prices, some of which might be attributed to
increased production, it is noteworthy there is not the equivalent
decline that marked pork prices. The element of stability wherein
mutton prices always were equal to those of beef possibly contributed to keep each producer from feeling superior to the other.
In other words, a dignity attended sheep ranching in earliest
New Spain that the early western United States did not know.

Indeed, one has strong reason to believe sheep ranching was
the more popular of the two in the earliest years. Whereas the
cabildo records of 1527-1528 bristle with frequent petitions for
and grants of land for sheep raising, it is rare indeed, in that
period, to find equivalent references to cattle raising. When a
conquistador like Ruy González came to engage in both sheep
and cattle raising, he not only inaugurated his ranching interest
with sheep but continued to raise them after he had turned to
cattle. An overwhelming majority of the brands registered before
1530 were for sheep, a lesser number were for cattle, and fewer
still served both purposes. Though some men, like Pedro Sánchez
Farfan and Ruy González, had separate brands, one for sheep
and one for cattle and horses, others, like García Holguín, used
a single brand on both cattle and sheep.

Most of the early sheep raisers grouped themselves together,
generally to the west of Mexico City. Beginning in the Chapultepec and Tacuba areas, the ranching properties stretched along
the two roads leading to Matalzingo. There, watered by the
Atengo River and backing up to the Sierra Matalzingo three or

so leagues from the capital, were the sheep-raising activities of numerous conquistadors, including Captain Gonzalo de Sandoval, brigantine skipper Juan Jaramillo—by now husband of the famous Indian Marina—shipbuilder Francisco Rodríguez, and Pedro Sánchez Farfan, who had seized Narváez in the coastal battle of 1520. An exception to this pattern was Antonio de Arriaga. A minor officer aboard a brigantine during the Battle of Tenochtitlán, Arriaga had his flock of sheep near Tepeyac, to the north of Mexico City.

Early ranching was not an activity reserved to persons of a single social or economic level. A cross section of the earliest ranchers proves the contrary. Along with, and literally alongside, powerful men like Captain Gonzalo de Sandoval, Treasurer Alonso de Estrada, Jorge Alvarado, García Holguín, military order commander Leonel de Cervantes, and Juan Jaramillo were locksmith Bartolomé González, gardener Alonso de Torres, blacksmith Juan de Yepez, carpenter Martín Pérez, tailor Juan Dávila, and the Negro Juan Hidalgo. An activity which later commanded the attention of viceroys, ranching meanwhile posed problems for municipal authorities as droves of livestock moved in and out of the city. The cabildo took steps to reduce the attendant nuisance, damage, and filth with a variety of penalties, including fines and confiscation of the offending animals.

Martín López was absent from the city at the moment the municipality finally decided to regulate livestock brands. His longtime friend and fellow conquistador from Seville, Lázaro Guerrero, filed the sheep brand which López and his partner Andrés Núñez had been using. The fact that López' partner was none other than the person who shared the encomienda of Tequixquiac with him suggests strongly that their ranching endeavor was in that district to the north of Mexico City. Perhaps Guerrero was merely doing an absent friend a favor as he registered the sheep brand—perhaps, too, as in days of the conquest, he was in the employ of López. Beginning with March 28, 1530, the brand registrations bore dates of issuance. Prior thereto, however, fifty-nine brands had been registered, among them that of López and Núñez. Seventeenth in the undated list of fifty-nine, it is assumed the registration was among the earliest, since the ordering of the names is without any arrangement other than a possible chronological one. For those who see double meaning in such matters, the simple, cross-shaped brand used by the shipwright could be considered an index to a religious nature.[10]

Upon his return to Mexico City from Tehuantepec in the autumn of 1529 the former alcalde mayor had more than property interests and commercial and ranching activities demanding his attention. The anti-Cortés audiencia had decided to level charges against Councilman Francisco de Santa Cruz, the one witness don Hernando had called in his legal battle of 1528 with López. About October 20, 1529, President Nuño de Guzmán and the audiencia ordered the arrest of Santa Cruz. Once Santa Cruz had been jailed, Prosecutor Juan de la Peña presented an indictment charging him with perjury. Probably unknown as yet in New Spain, the crown on August 24, 1529, had ordered royal officials to proceed against perjurors with full vigor of the law. A fine of 10,000 maravedis was established.[11] Detailing the instances in which Santa Cruz had perjured himself in his testimony supporting Cortés in the López suit, the prosecutor asked the court to adjudge Santa Cruz guilty and to condemn him to maximum penalties, both civil and criminal.[12] In addition, de la Peña urged that the defendant's property be sequestrated and that Santa Cruz himself be confined. On October 30 the prisoner was released on bail of one thousand pesos.

Opening phases of the case, vigorously blunt in the show of ill will between prosecutor and defendant, left no doubt that this

[10] *Actas de cabildo*, I, 6, 57, 58, 72, 80, 81, 129, 131, 133, 136, 139, 142, 151, 158, 159, 161, 162-63, 165, 176-77, 180, 183; II, 3, 16, 21, 196-201; Millares Carlo and Mantecón, *Indice y extractos*, I, nos. 15, 477, 478, 605, 1024, 1259, 1616, 1726.

[11] Vasco de Puga, *Provisiones, Cedulas, Instrucciones para el gobierno de la Nueva España*, Colección de Incunables Americanos Siglo XVI, vol. III (Madrid, 1945), fol. 70.

[12] The record of this litigation is in López, 1529-1550, pp. 1-57, Conway Coll. (LC).

was a contest between the old and new orders in New Spain. Santa Cruz' counsel was none other than attorney Altamirano, who had engineered Cortés' defense against López in 1528.

The López-Cortés proceedings of 1528 were incorporated into the record. Then Santa Cruz presented an eighteen-item inter-rogatory and called for testimony from thirteen witnesses. This document featured an attack upon the character of the prosecutor and fulsome praise for the defendant. More than two-thirds of it belittled the brigantine building and the shipwright, with particular derision heaped upon Martín López.

The following men constituted Santa Cruz' list of witnesses: Alonso Arévalo, Francisco de Vargas, Martín de Motrico, Ruy González, Juan Tirado, Andrés López, Miguel Diez, Francisco García, Diego Hernández, Luis Infante, Gonzalo Cerezo, Gonzalo Rodríguez de Ocano, and Juan Rodríguez de Villafuerte. With the exception of Martín de Motrico, all were veterans of the warfare of 1521, and three of them had known duty with the navy. Motrico was called obviously because he could offer a professional opinion regarding the wages of shipbuilders, since he was a master maker of masts with workmen in his employ in Vera Cruz. His testimony on wage scales after the fighting days was introduced as a fair appraisal of the wartime conditions, about which he personally knew nothing.

All in all the testimony of thirteen witnesses hurt Martín López considerably and helped him not in the least when his personal fortunes were so drawn into the maelstrom of colonial political warfare by the unresolved Santa Cruz—de la Peña case.

In late 1529 another court action was imminent. The im-prisoned Maldonado knew a fury which might have produced immediate action if he could have obtained release from the prison of the audiencia. Also giving him pause was the continued control of New Spain by his enemies of the first audiencia, as well as the absence of his leader, now a marquis, who was not to return to New Spain until the next year. Before then, circumstances swept López out of Mexico City once more.

In the autumn of 1529 it was evident that another political

shift had occurred. The audiencia headed by Nuño de Guzmán was declining in prestige and power. While rebuilding his own position to some degree in Spain (this was the interval in which he became marquis of the Valley of Oaxaca as one token of the esteem in which the crown continued to hold him), Cortés undermined Nuño de Guzmán. A short-term, but nonetheless powerful, ally of Cortés in this assault upon the audiencia was Bishop Zumárraga. Few battles on the church-state level in three centuries of Spanish rule in America rival the no-holds-barred struggle between Guzmán and Zumárraga, a fight which incidentally did much to consolidate previously bickering and divided churchmen. So markedly had Guzmán's position deteriorated by late 1529 that something was required to reestablish his name, while diverting attention from a struggle in which he was something less than winner. As Cortés had gone to Honduras in 1524 and worsened his position, so Guzmán's campaign into New Galicia was destined to hurt him further.

It was a highly charged and changing atmosphere in which López found himself in Mexico City that autumn, with his suit against Cortés reactivated by virtue of the Santa Cruz perjury case, with the threat of litigation directed at him by Maldonado, with settlement of his wife's estate, and with newly gained information that Cortés was a property-holding neighbor of his in downtown Mexico City.[13] In addition there was the excitement attending the recruitment of a following for Guzmán's projected campaign into New Galicia.

[13] Pacheco and others, XII, 376-77; XXIX, 331.

## CHAPTER VII

# FROM AUDIENCIA TO AUDIENCIA

HEN in his early forties, Martín López was forced into Nuño de Guzmán's military ranks in late 1529.[1] The compulsion to which López yielded seems to have been born of complex circumstances. The deteriorating position of Guzmán, plus competing demands upon the limited Spanish manpower then in Mexico City, possibly forced the president of the audiencia to draft some men for his campaign. Having cast his lot earlier with the audiencia, López was compelled to continue in Guzmán's camp or face the prospect of being stripped of his property, a potent measure repeatedly employed in that period. López, recently identified with Guzmán's government, must also have known that former Guzmán appointees who remained behind in Mexico City might expect the full fury of irate successors, and felt it highly desirable to let a little time elapse before resettling permanently in Mexico City.

Furthermore, it was apparent to López that the successful outcome
of his litigation probably depended on Guzmán's success and
retention of authority. Two other circumstances which might
partially explain the drafting of López concern his unmarried
status and his financial well-being.

At his own expense, eventually involving more than 10,000
pesos of his personal fortune, López outfitted and supported
himself and his servants for the campaign that consumed approximately two years. With him went an undisclosed number of
Spanish servants, two Negro servants, and five or six horses, all
of which called for considerable outlay of cash in 1529. The
price of a Negro slave in 1527-1528 commonly had ranged
between 100 and 300 gold pesos. One year before López left for
New Galicia the prices of horses in Mexico City, though varying
widely, averaged in excess of 100 gold pesos.[2] Even more significant than the initial cost of horses and Negro slaves was the expense of maintaining them over a two-year period. Most revealing
at that time as an indication of López' wealth was his ability to
maintain Spanish servants. Of unknown extent and derived from
a combination of sources, the López estate stemmed from booty,
municipal grants, ranching and encomienda income, commercial
and mining ventures, and his deceased wife's property.

Few major sixteenth-century campaigns conducted by Spaniards in the New World are attended by such vagueness as char-
acterizes the accounts of the Guzmán expedition into New Galicia.
No agreement exists concerning the date of departure from
Mexico City, nor the time when most of the men returned. No
agreement exists concerning the number of men involved; nor
can clear statements of the itineraries of the main force or of any
of its subsidiary groups be made. Yet amid all this confusion,

[1] López, 1528-1574, pp. 63, 150, 170, 179, 183, Conway Coll. (Aberdeen);
López, 1529-1550, pp. 124, 132, 139, 154, 160-61, 167, Conway Coll. (LC).
[2] López, 1528-1574, pp. 63, 115, 122, 150, Conway Coll. (Aberdeen); López,
1529-1550, pp. 124, 132, 139, 147, 154, 160-61, 167, Conway Coll. (LC); Millares
Carlo and Mantecón, *Indice y extractos*, I, nos. 401, 593, 626a, 665, 736, 862,
885, 907, 994, 1117, 1139, 1214, 1254, 1314, 1387, 1498, 1556, 1609, 1685, 1706,
1733, 1735, 1741, 1750, 1755, 1768, 1769, 1788.

the needless barbarity attending the expedition emerges crystal clear. The tone of the New Galicia campaign derived primarily from the barbarous nature which Guzmán had already exhibited in the Pánuco region on the Gulf coast; the men in the ranks, like López, who had fought and lived with the natives for years without exhibiting such brutality, had no reason to adopt it in New Galicia except that the nature of their leader thrust it upon them—as, indeed, he had thrust much of the desperate madness of this entire period upon them.

The Spanish contingent in the force numbered between about 300 and somewhat more than 500 men. Among fifteen notables in Guzmán's ranks listed by Mota, Martín López is conspicuously absent. A staff list of thirty-one constructed by López-Portillo, which includes all subordinates of Guzmán with any command function from deputy commander down to guide, likewise omits Martín López, who appears in the general list of horsemen and foot soldiers.[3] Lacking any command function and finding himself among a throng of 200 horsemen, López had a rather ordinary role in this expedition which counted many times the number of cavalrymen commanded by Cortés in 1519-1521. Among his colleagues in arms, he could count such acquaintances as Juan Griego Girón, Andrés López, Juan de Zamudio, Gonzalo Cerezo, Martín Monje, Andrés Núñez, Pedro de Villanueva, and Alonso de Contreras, all veterans of the Cortés-led conquest.

The last named, Alonso de Contreras, possibly typified many of the followers of Guzmán in more than one respect. Originally with the Narváez band, Contreras had spent a decade in the land, during which time he had loyally served Cortés. After the fall of Tenochtitlán he had spent additional months in the campaigns radiating from the Valley of Mexico. When Olid's expedition was being readied for Honduras, Contreras served as the agent of Cortés in Cuba procuring necessary supplies. Finally Contreras

---

[3] José López-Portillo y Weber, *La conquista de la Nueva Galicia* (Mexico City, 1935), 120-28, suggests the lesser number; Matías de la Mota y Padilla, *Historia de la conquista del Reino de la Nueva Galicia*, ed. by José Ireneo Gutierrez (Guadalajara, 1920), 40, offers the greater figure.

became disgruntled, for he had had to await the arrival of the first audiencia before receiving his initial grant of an encomienda. Then he was called upon to serve with Guzmán. Unable to refuse lest the grant be rescinded, Contreras poured time, effort, and means into the New Galicia campaign. As he joined Nuño de Guzmán's military expedition, he brought to it three horses, one servant, two Negroes, and arms—in all an investment of more than 2,000 gold pesos.[4] Obviously López was not alone in the nature and extent of his contribution to the Guzmán venture.

On the verge of leaving Mexico City for an indeterminate period, López conferred his power of attorney upon a fellow resident, Hernán Medel. Time was to prove to López that the trust he put in Medel was misplaced.

Why López selected Medel as the recipient of a power of attorney which made him master over the López estate cannot be explained fully. Many of his earlier conquistador and neighborhood acquaintances were absent from Mexico City, others were dead. Moreover, some of the men he once might have considered for such a responsibility were now aligned too completely with the interests of crown or Cortés to appeal to him, or him to them for that matter. For a variety of reasons, López probably was forced to turn from consideration of many whose interests and abilities suggested they might successfully administer his property.

Hernán Medel was one of the rank and file among conquistadors who did little or nothing meriting distinction in war or peace. Late in 1525 he held property and possibly resided some distance east of Martín López, between the principal plaza of Mexico City and the arsenal in which the brigantines were sheltered. Medel's activities of the late 1520's suggest a range of interests typical of many Spaniards in Mexico City at the time. He was part owner of a gang of 150 Indian slaves; and on several

---

[4] López-Portillo y Weber, 122, 125, 126; López, 1528-1574, pp. 115, 122, 128, Conway Coll. (Aberdeen); Información de los méritos y servicios de Pedro de Villanueva (1554), Paso y Troncoso Coll., Leg. 97; Información de los méritos y servicios de Alonso de Contreras (1531), *ibid.*, Leg. 93.

occasions he served individuals as their authorized debt-collecting agent, a commonplace activity in a day so lacking in the money and banking facilities now taken for granted. Medel's horse-trading activities found him often a debtor, occasionally a creditor. His commercial transactions repeatedly included the buying and selling of houses and slaves.

Reading a bit between the lines, one suspects that a combination of certain of Medel's activities of 1528 tended to recommend him to López' attention the following year. On January 14, 1528, Medel turned for legal counsel to attorney Francisco de Alva. López and Núñez had done likewise the previous week. If Medel's recourse to the same attorney at almost the same moment had behind it the same reasons—disgruntlement and hostility toward Cortés—López had a sympathetic fellow conquistador holding his power of attorney at the end of 1529.

Medel, desiring his wife, sent Bartolomé Hernández to Palos for her in mid-October, 1528. During Hernández' absence from the New World, Medel administered his Indians and other property. Out of this Medel might have emerged a more settled citizen of Mexico City, with wife at hand to lend greater stability to his household. His handling of Hernández' affairs during the months immediately prior to López' departure for service in Tehuantepec likewise might have favorably impressed the former shipwright. Medel obviously was a man of some means and much energy. Perhaps it is wrong to question López' choice of the man simply because the absence of records suggests he and López were without previous significant business or social connections. Indeed, López might have preferred the administration of his property by one with whom he knew only an impersonal business relationship. At any rate, Hernán Medel was the man to whom López granted an all-encompassing power of attorney before he mustered with the Guzmán force and moved in the direction of New Galicia.[5]

[5] *Actas de cabildo,* I, 62; Millares Carlo and Mantecón, I, nos. 399, 767, 795, 861, 884, 890, 953, 1003, 1009, 1158, 1285, 1392, 1417, 1501, 1591, 1658, 1659, 1660.

The Christmas season of 1529 saw the Guzmán-led group, including Martín López, his servants, horses, and arms, inaugurate a campaign in a vast region west and northwest of Mexico City. Into areas like Michoacán, Colima, and Jalisco, whose initial conquests had been engineered by Cortés-sponsored expeditions, Guzmán pushed, fought battles, seized native leaders as hostages, tortured and enslaved defeated Indians. Like a plague, Guzmán insinuated fear into native hearts. Ever west and north he and his men moved, beyond Lake Chapala to the Pacific coast, along which they campaigned for hundreds of miles.

Confusion in time and space befog our knowledge of the expedition. From certain places divisions fanned out on subsidiary reconnaissances and conquests. Native towns were burned and left behind, and the native rumor of an island of Amazons inspired a search as lustful as it was unsuccessful. Refusing to answer the summons of the second audiencia in Mexico City, Guzmán remained distant and negotiated directly and successfully with the crown for recognition of his authority in New Galicia. A fearsome scourge upon the natives, a flaunter of authority, and a founder of towns, Nuño de Guzmán, before his ranks thinned through deaths and departures, did much to extend Spanish interest northwest of present-day Jalisco.

Despite all that is recorded against Guzmán, it must be said for him that he was a man of great energy. Often misused or sorely misdirected in leadership, Indian relations, and many other matters, Guzmán's energy was needed to face the famines, the floods, the plagues, and the native strategies which appeared time and time again. One can be elated by the hardihood of Spaniards which permitted them to face frightful physical obstacles—as great as those Cortés knew. One can be depressed by the miserable quality of leadership, wherein little or no similarity can be drawn between Guzmán and Cortés.

In the career of one man, the New Galicia campaign did little more than add two years to his age and subtract more than ten thousand pesos from his pocket. In the course of two years with

Guzmán, López probably traveled greater distances than in an equivalent period with Cortés.

Aside from the general triumph over space and hardship which characterized an experience that ever after must have called to López' mind nightmarish memories, the man as an individual emerges, or seems to emerge, on several occasions, still the artisan-soldier. Desiring to commemorate the triumph north of Lake Chapala at Tonalán early in March, 1530, the campaigners erected a cross and a church. Martín López took charge of the Indians assigned to the undertaking. The pretty little church drew no special plaudits from the chroniclers of the campaign, but the cross was quite unusual. Standing sixty feet high, it could be seen from a distance of more than four leagues. This project at Tonalán, ironically commemorating the inhumanity of Guzmán, consumed about fifteen days.[6]

On no other occasion does López emerge from the ranks in the course of two years, though one strongly senses his presence in a minor episode involving amphibious operations. Shortly before the victory at Tonalán, the Spanish force was pinned down on a riverbank at Ocotlán by heavy enemy fire which prohibited their crossing. Taking a leaf from the Lake Texcoco experience a decade earlier, some rafts were constructed which, spearheaded by men with slings, enabled the Spaniards to assault the Indian position successfully.[7] A far cry from the full-blown navy of cannon-bearing brigantines, the operation of 1530 so calls to mind events of 1520-1521 as to make it seem possible López was also a party to this second episode.

One day at Chiametla, close to the Pacific Ocean and to the north of Aztatlán on his way to Culiacán, Nuño de Guzmán evidenced considerable interest in shipping. On January 18, 1531, the discredited president of the audiencia ordered Francisco Verdugo and Andrés Núñez to lead ventures in the province of Zacatula, where they were to locate and complete two brigantines

---

[6] Pacheco and others, *Colección de documentos inéditos,* XIII, 374; XIV, 354.
[7] Mota y Padilla, 50.

already under construction. Once the ships were finished, command of them would devolve upon Andrés Núñez.[8]

Concerning these activities for which he was so singularly qualified, no reference is made to Martín López. In Verdugo, Nuño de Guzmán was entrusting the project to one of his principal captains, the man who served also as treasurer of the New Galicia expedition. Verdugo had served aboard a brigantine during the siege of Tenochtitlán and thereafter had figured in the foremost ranks of anti-Cortés men in New Spain. His identification with the shipping schemes of Guzmán attests the importance the commander of the expedition put upon the vessels. In Andrés Núñez, friend, partner, and neighbor of Martín López, Guzmán was turning to an experienced brigantine builder and captain of the 1520-1521 era. Why López was not connected with this Zacatula project is not known.

Quite possibly Martín López the hidalgo shipwright, servant-attended horseman, and reluctant recruit who had marched to Tzintzuntzan, Tonalán, Nochistlán, Tepic, Aztatlán, and other points far to the northwest of the Valley of Mexico, was even then en route to still-changing Mexico City. In a confused two-year campaign the role of Martín López is so imperfectly established that his service in New Galicia defies accurate evaluation. Mixed motives had led to his identification with Guzmán; and mixed motives probably led to his departure from Guzmán. The conquistador who returned to Mexico City out of the northwest was still acquisitive and selfish enough to want to recover his estate; and he was noble enough to disengage himself from Guzmán's rapacity and greed, and decent enough to face the criticism and condemnation new royal authorities might heap upon him. Far from simple when he departed Mexico City, López was an equally complex personality as he returned there.

The opening years of the 1530's saw the coming of the much-awaited second audiencia to New Spain. In Bishop Fuenleal the new government had competent direction from an experienced

8 Paso y Troncoso, *Epistolario de Nueva España*, II, 10-11.

administrator who, unlike Guzmán, was without worldly ambitions. Returning to New Spain with the new audiencia was Captain General Hernando Cortés, now marquis of the Valley of Oaxaca. Cortés' friendly relations with the second audiencia became another harbinger of stability for New Spain. There were numerous other factors, such as the strength of the church under Bishop Zumárraga, the removal of many of the most unsettled elements from Mexico City, and the general weariness of the Spanish population in the land, to promote the transition experienced by New Spain in the early thirties and to end a restless, striving decade the like of which New Spain was never to know again.

The new audiencia began its duties by conducting the residencia of its predecessor, a procedure which was colored by the continued absence of Nuño de Guzmán, who seemed fully aware of the fact his record in general and the conquest of New Galicia in particular gave rise to much damaging criticism. Better treatment of the Indians, a major emphasis now, involved the termination of certain encomiendas by the new administration. Among the more than one hundred men affected by the crown's policy was Martín López. Humanitarian policies aroused hostility by preventing citizens of San Estevan del Puerto in the Pánuco area from shipping Indian slaves to Caribbean island settlements in exchange for horses and cattle. Similar reaction to the new Indian policy came from the Guzmán-founded town of Compostela in New Galicia.[9] However, the immensity of New Spain, a continuing obstacle to good administration, also prevented rapid coalescence of opposition.

Everywhere—on the Gulf and Pacific coasts as well as in the interior—the conquistadors were losing their fight to use as they might the inhabitants of the land they had conquered, but they nonetheless continued the struggle, by communities, groups, and individuals. While some men voiced their complaints to the nearest town council or within the colonial courts, others unhesitatingly appealed directly to Spain. One who employed this

[9] *Ibid.*, I, 153-66; II, 36; III, 32-34.

technique was Gerónimo López, a veteran of the Tenochtitlán fighting as well as subsequent campaigning on both the Gulf and Pacific coasts. Some of his petitioning had resulted in 1530 in the royal grant of a coat of arms to him and his descendants, a form of reward to which many conquistadors eventually turned. A bit more than a year later, in mid-1531, Gerónimo was complaining directly to his king that in the midst of a land rich with possibilities he, without Indians, could make nothing of that opportunity. The appeal smacks of the tone of another conquistador, one recently stripped of some of his Indians. The Seville shipwright's conquistador-shoemaker acquaintance Hernando de Cantillana was another who appealed directly to the throne for an allotment of Indians.[10]

The second audiencia bore instructions emphasizing certain royal aims. Along with attention to the natives, it was charged, too, with trying to reform the conquistadors. Extravagance in dress and living drew renewed attention. Gambling caused the crown to strive to enforce earlier laws. Since the first days of the conquest, gambling for high stakes had been a daily activity in New Spain, and the second audiencia had the same instructions given it as royal agent Luis Ponce and the first audiencia.[11]

This peaceful new day merely served to return Martín López in the 1530's to the courts; but first some readjustments were in order.

As he neared Mexico City on his return from the two-year campaign in New Galicia, the conquistador must have looked forward to better days. The duty with Nuño de Guzmán had been wearying, unproductive, and expensive in what was to prove his last military campaign. The New Galicia duty had not given distinction to López. Possibly he felt the best way to forget the recent campaign would be to press once more his case involving the unrewarded services of the earlier period. With a new political administration in Mexico City, the resurrection of the case against

---

[10] *Ibid.*, II, 2-6, 107-109, 141-42.
[11] Puga, *Provisiones, Cedulas, Instrucciones*, fols. 23v, 42v, 67r, 70v-71r.

Cortés well might be his first concern. First, that is, after he had relieved Hernán Medel of the power of attorney accorded him.

The miseries of fruitless fighting were as naught compared with the pain López knew when he learned that in his absence he had been impoverished by the malicious Medel. The extent of his losses mirrors better than any other available information the measure of his wealth.

Medel had sold, squandered, and otherwise consumed a large segment of López' total wealth. A group of buildings one short block from the principal plaza of Mexico City, on the west side of the juncture of the present-day streets of Moneda and Licenciado Verdad, had constituted the principal downtown property holding of the former shipwright. On his return from New Galicia, López learned that they had become the episcopal residence, sold to Bishop-designate Zumárraga by Medel on March 21, 1530, for 1,200 pesos.[12]

This sale, taking place less than three months after Martín López' departure, suggests Medel had dishonest intentions from the outset. But in view of the impending wrath of Francisco Maldonado, López might have instructed his agent to convert his estate to cash, which would be easier to conceal should a court render judgment against him. However, agent Medel not only disposed of the property, but also the income derived from its sale, and he went on victimizing the distant and unsuspecting López. Five gardening plots, constituting a single, large market-gardening site in the district between Chapultepec and Coyoacán, were also converted to cash, which Medel promptly spent for his own purposes. Having sold buildings, he did not hesitate to sell the miscellaneous goods he found stored therein. In such fashion the jewelry, numerous gold and silver ornaments, and the furniture belonging to Martín López were disposed of. Medel also sold López' share in the 130 Indian slaves in the vicinity of

---

[12] Joaquín García Icazbalceta, *Don Fray Juan de Zumárraga—Primer Obispo y Arzobispo de México*, ed. by Rafael Aguayo Spencer and Antonio Castro Leal (4 vols., Mexico City, 1947), I, 196; II, 256-61, 309-10; IV, 86.

Olinalá which the conquistador owned in partnership with Alonso de Aguilar. Such groups of natives, often exploited in mining in the late 1520's, commanded between six and seven gold pesos per Indian when sold in lots of 100, as was the common practice.[13]

From the proceeds of successive sales of buildings, land, jewelry, home furnishings, and Indians, Medel stole considerably more than 20,000 pesos. Yet the money-mad Medel went even further. In his absence, Martín López' share of the estate of his deceased parents had been converted into merchandise and shipped to New Spain. (With the original manuscript missing, confusion enters at this point. For one thing, López' father was alive and fighting in Spanish courts after this date. Perhaps the reference is to Martín López' wife, or possibly even her parents.) On its arrival at Vera Cruz, royal officials had valued the shipment at 11,700 pesos. With goods in great demand, prices high, and the experienced López capable of capitalizing on conditions, such merchandise represented a market value considerably in excess of that customhouse declaration. As soon as the goods reached Vera Cruz, Medel hurried to sell them, pocketing and spending the cash he received. In all, the value of the property Medel misappropriated from López exceeded 40,000 pesos. To make a bad matter worse, the villainous spendthrift died intestate. The death of Medel cannot be dated, but the fact that he was alive as late as April 2, 1531, when he, as López' agent, was named defendant in a legal action, clearly indicated Martín López was absent from Mexico City more than sixteen months before he returned from New Galicia.[14]

How bitter must have been the return of campaign-weary López! His fortune was gone, and he could not recover the losses from the estate of the deceased Medel. Three decades later, worn and in want, López recounted this phase of his career, stating that upon his return from New Galicia he was a ruined man. As a final blow, on his return to Mexico City, Martín López

[13] Millares Carlo and Mantecón, I, nos. 1381, 1688.
[14] Maldonado contra López, I, 71, 112, Conway Coll. (Cambridge).

learned that somewhat more than fifty Indian slaves employed in a silver-mining enterprise in Sultepec had been freed by order of the second audiencia.[15]

López was probably present for the entrance of the president of the second audiencia late in September, 1531. To greet the eminent churchman and royal administrator, the municipal council ordered the citizenry to ride forth to receive him. Trumpeters added their special acclaim. On the street leading to Iztapalapa, by which the official was to enter, three large arches had been erected. Even the Indians of the city were instructed to attend the welcoming festivities.[16] Along with other disgruntled conquistadors who were pursuing a wait-and-see attitude, López was likely astride a horse and a party to the fanfare that ushered in the last and strongest figure of the new regime.

Meanwhile, in January, 1530—shortly after he had set out for New Galicia—Martín López' father and two uncles had initiated a prolonged court battle in Spain concerning their social status. Starting with the addition of their names to the tax list of Seville as tax-evading commoners, the case saw the trio successfully prove their knightly and tax-exempt status, thanks in part to vigorous testimony from eleven witnesses drawn from various regions of Spain. Since the final decision was not handed down until the summer of 1533, this litigation was still alive when the former shipwright journeyed to his mother country, in 1532, for one or more reasons: legal matters connected with his wife Inés' death, affairs related to the kinsman's estate that had so assisted Medel's self-enrichment program, or a search for a woman of quality as a second wife.[17]

More important in the life of Martín López than the affair of family position was his marriage to Juana Hernández. This son of Seville, himself a hidalgo, took in marriage a daughter of that city of equivalent social position. Basing their married life in

[15] López, 1528-1574, pp. 155, 160, 164, 169, 173, 186, Conway Coll. (Aberdeen).
[16] *Actas de cabildo*, II, 78, 130.
[17] Misc. Docs., 5-41, Conway Coll. (Cambridge).

Mexico City, the proud Martín and his Juana of gentle birth and unblemished descent proceeded to establish an honorable household and a large family of which they and their acquaintances were proud throughout succeeding decades.

No facet of Martín López' very long and full life is more difficult to trace than that which marks him a husband, a father, a neighbor. Military careers are repeatedly and rather fully stated in verified statements of services executed by many of the surviving warriors; political careers can be traced through cabildo records, royal cedulas, and records of visitas and residencias; economic interests of individuals are evident in shares of booty, municipal land grants, encomiendas, and innumerable legal documents executed before notaries. But there is little record of the social life of any person in New Spain.

It is thought that Martín López and his wife Juana had ten children, five boys and five girls, with the oldest a boy born in 1533.[18] The first-born, Martín López Ossorio, had not only his father's name but also that of his noble family of the homeland. Young Martín López Ossorio was to bear increasingly his father's hopes as years passed on, figuring in petitions which sought opportunities and honors for the son of the conquistador as well as for the brigantine builder himself. As the senior male heir, more is known of Martín López Ossorio than of any of his brothers and sisters.

Of young Martín's four brothers, three can be identified. Not necessarily in order of birth, they were Agustín, Pedro, and Bernabé, all of whom served as clergymen in New Spain. One boy is outside the range of recognition by name or later occupation. The unfortunate fifth son in a family that had too little to bequeath even a first-born must be relegated to historical oblivion.

In the mean little first cathedral of Mexico City—made to appear all the more so because of the noble dimensions of the plaza on which it fronted—Agustín López was baptized by Padre

[18] López, 1528-1574, pp. 63, 72, 90, 106, 148-49, 157, 161, 165, 169, 174, 178, 182, Conway Coll. (Aberdeen); López, 1529-1550, pp. 123, 131-32, 139, 147, 160, 167, Conway Coll. (LC); Martín López Ossorio, 92, *ibid.*

Bachiller Diego Rodríguez on September 7, 1540. Four god-parents were beside mother, father, and son at the moment of baptism.

Another son, Bernabé, appears in the baptismal register under date of June 18, 1547. Like his brother Agustín seven years earlier, he was baptized by Padre Rodríguez. Three godparents stood on this occasion with Martín, Juana, and their infant son.[19]

Although none of the births of the other seven children can be assigned to definite years, the information that Juana bore a child as late as 1547 indicates that the second wife was considerably younger than the husband in that household, for the conquistador father was between 57 and 60 years of age when Bernabé was born.

If vagueness attends four sons and utter obscurity engulfs the other one, the daughters are even less fortunate. Only the eldest one can be named, and the haze enveloping her gives way to abysmal ignorance regarding her quartet of nameless sisters. Father had been honored in the naming of the eldest son, and in like fashion, mother was remembered when the oldest daughter was given the name Juana. Proof that Juana was among the oldest of all the children is seen in her marriage sometime prior to 1560.[20]

By 1533 it was to the founding of this family that López turned many of his energies, and in so doing, he, his wife, and the house-hold they maintained played a part in the introduction and stabilization of Spanish culture in New Spain. Meanwhile, other circumstances, beyond the power of Martín López, had helped calm down long-tempestuous New Spain.

The five experienced administrators of the second audiencia speedily stabilized New Spain. Many have unfairly denied the second audiencia the credit it deserves. Not without justice did Friar Luis de Fuensalida, Franciscan superior in Mexico City, praise the second audiencia for its administration, the merino

---

[19] Libro 1° de bautisimos de la cathedral, desde noviembre de 1536 hasta octubre de 1547, fols. 63, 187 (Archivo de la Catedral, Mexico City). Appreciation is directed to Jorge Ignacio Rubio Mañé of the Archivo General de la Nación who supplemented the author's search of these records.
[20] López, 1528-1574, p. 153, Conway Coll. (Aberdeen).

sheep, and the olive trees that had been introduced into the land.

An audiencia led by churchmen created an atmosphere favorable to Christian missionary work.[21] Along with reorganization of bishoprics and the provinces of the regular clergy occurred a significant event, in 1532, which hastened native acceptance of Christianity. The revelation of the Virgin Mary to the humble Indian Juan Diego, reinforced by a likeness of the mother of Jesus in hues that unmistakably identified her with the Indian race, sped native conversions. Soon the Virgin of Guadalupe, special object of Indian affection and veneration, became the patron saint of all New Spain.

Conquistadors less than enthusiastic about the second audiencia often cooperated with it, as at Puebla. Founded in the earliest thirties as an intermediate point between Mexico City and Vera Cruz, Puebla was unique among early Spanish settlements in having no previous Indian community as its nucleus; hence it had an unusually strong Spanish atmosphere. To help disperse the hard core of conquistadors who were a continuing obstacle to royal intentions, special inducements were offered, not least of which was exemption for thirty years from the sales tax and the ancient levy termed the *pecho,* which inclined more than one to take up residence in Puebla.[22]

During these years of the second audiencia, the shipwright-conquistador from Seville was busy once more in the colonial judiciary. By 1531 Francisco Maldonado was no longer in prison. The coming of the second audiencia, the return of Cortés to New Spain, and López' absence in New Galicia had improved Maldonado's position.

The Maldonado-López litigation falls into a series of interrupted actions lasting more than a decade, all of them confused and devoid of definitive decision. Maldonado challenged the results of the residencia to which he had submitted and sought damages from López for his arrest and imprisonment and the

21 Paso y Troncoso, II, 33-35, 125-27.
22 *Ibid.,* 111; III, 137-44.

seizure of his personal property (valued at 10,000 gold pesos).

What had happened to Maldonado's property following the inventories and sequestrations of 1529 is an unanswered question. It seems unlikely—though not inconceivable—that López seized some of it for his personal gain. Compounding the confusion is the possibility that Maldonado had been fined by the audiencia, with that body seizing his property in payment. If this be true, Maldonado had no reason for suing López except for personal bodily abuse. However, with Guzmán beyond the judicial arm of Mexico City authorities, one suspects that a case rightly to be directed against the first audiencia was, on the basis of availability rather than liability, directed at López.

From the standpoint of the larger interests of Cortés, Maldonado also was concerned about certain Indians, uncollected tribute, and the Tehuantepec ships. Accordingly, López was named defendant in a number of separate but related suits inaugurated by Maldonado and Cortés.

At last López, on October 21, 1533, replied to the allegations of Maldonado, denying the charges. The plaintiff countered with a repetition of his individual charges against López, and he also belittled the former shipwright's services during the conquest and demanded that López be subjected to a residencia covering his tenure of office in Tehuantepec. Late 1533 and the early months of 1534 found both parties fattening the court proceedings as they gathered evidence in Antequera.

On March 20, 1534, López' agent presented to the officials in Compostela, New Galicia, the necessary authorizations from the audiencia along with a request for testimony from Francisco del Barco. During López' Tehuantepec experience, del Barco had gone there as majordomo and tax collector.[23] By the end of the year, however, inaction set in, and before the suit was reactivated, the government of the first viceroy had succeeded that of the second audiencia.[24]

[23] Misc. Docs., 93-109, Conway Coll. (Cambridge); Hospital de Jesús, 300/107.
[24] Maldonado contra López, I, 1-20, 24-62, 122-40; II, 1-3, 5-41, 50-66; III, 83-97; IV, 14-21, Conway Coll. (Cambridge).

Even as Maldonado and Cortés tenaciously pursued their cases against Martín López, the shipwright must have felt that with a new administration came new hope—why not a new effort? So it happened in 1534, mid the snarl of his litigation with Maldonado and Cortés over affairs of Tehuantepec dated 1529, that Martín López again went to the courts regarding issues recalling Tenochtitlán, Tlaxcala, and Texcoco of 1519, 1520, and 1521.[25]

The López-instigated litigation of 1534 differed from that of 1528 primarily in minor aspects of the interrogatory he employed and in some of the witnesses he called. Whereas the interrogatory of 1528 contained thirteen queries, that of 1534 had thirty-seven. Subjectwise, the interrogatory of 1534 not only included the three shipbuilding episodes but also added a considerable block of evidence regarding the personal services of López in many areas, both before and after the fall of Tenochtitlán.

The witnesses of 1534 and 1528 were alike in that both groups were veterans of the fighting of 1521. Ten of sixteen men in 1528 were literate; in 1534 only five of ten were so designated. Of the 1528 witnesses, fourteen of the sixteen had worked with López among the shipbuilders; the second group included but six men who had worked with the shipwright. Five of the ten men answering questions for López in 1534-1535 had served aboard the brigantines during the fighting of mid-1521. Naturally the witnesses in the second court action were older than the first group, but they were, like the earlier witnesses, a combination of artisans and unknowns. Four men gave testimony on both occasions—Lázaro Guerrero, Diego Ramírez, Juan Gómez de Herrera, and Alvar López. Two of these were illiterate; three were carpenters; one was an unknown.

The great stumbling block in López' case of 1528 had been his placing of precise peso values upon his role in each of the three shipbuilding programs. Remembering that he had won in principle, only to lose out when the issue of specific award had been

25 The record of this court action is in López, 1528-1574, pp. 57-143, Conway Coll. (Aberdeen).

assigned to six referees, López did not ask for specific sums in 1534. The plaintiff said that in 1519-1521 the wage of a ship-wright was eight gold pesos per day. Witness Guerrero promptly insisted that López "deserved more than fifteen for the excellence of his work and the fact that he did the work of three carpenters, to say the least." Lázaro Guerrero recalled hearing Cortés tell López that the shipwright merited the title of count or duke.

New in the 1534 statement of the case was López' account of the role of the brigantines in the siege of Tenochtitlán. Herein he amended the incomplete and modest interrogatory of 1528. After a detailed and convincing account of the building and operation of the brigantines, López closed with these statements: "the principal means whereby the city was taken were the brigan-tines and without them the city would not have been taken"; and "at the time the brigantines were built there was no person in the land capable of building them other than Martín López."

Every witness acknowledged the indispensability of the ships in the capture of Tenochtitlán, often in particularly poignant terms, and everyone supported the former shipwright's contention that his contribution was as unique as it was essential. Lázaro Guerrero, himself a brigantine builder, compared López with the other shipbuilders in these words: "the other skilled workmen available were mere carpenters, incapable of designing and super-intending the construction, as he [López] had done, and without his financial resources and his tools, not to speak of his energy and zeal." Simply and unequivocally Juan Gómez de Herrera declared that "if it had not been for Martín López, the vessels would not have been built and the Spaniards would have been hard put to it to retake the capital."

In adding many details concerning other phases of his own fifteen-year career in New Spain, López' anger toward Cortés was evident when he charged his former commander with having rendered an account to the throne concerning 30,000 pesos he falsely claimed to have expended on the construction of the brigantines of the conquest. In the light of his own inability to collect for bona fide services and expenditures, López must have been particularly irritated by Cortés' efforts to collect something for nothing. One López witness of 1534, Diego Ramírez, traced the story of Cortés' claim for such remuneration to Licenciado Delgadillo, a member of the first audiencia. If, in truth, this difficult-to-trace claim did originate during the days of the first audiencia, it well could have played a significant part in inspiring the second suit by López.

Fellow conquistadors supported López' assertion that his encomienda was one of the smallest and poorest in the land, describing it as a handful of lazy, poverty-ridden, squalid, worthless Indians whose annual tribute payment to López was between sixty and one hundred pesos. Such, in their opinion, amounted to shabby reward for one who had contributed so signally to the victory at Tenochtitlán

The second suit by the former shipwright was no more successful than the effort of 1528. The year 1534 was a bad moment for the initiation of long-continuing litigation, though it undoubtedly looked good to López because the second audiencia seemed unusually stable. Actually, however, the second audiencia was but an interim administration, it having been determined much earlier that New Spain was shortly to become a viceroyalty. Officials who knew themselves to be in such a delicate and temporary position were hardly ones to resolve major snarls. In turn the government of the first viceroy easily resorted to procrastination when episodes out of the troubled past dangled before it.

Identification with the discredited first audiencia surely did not help the former shipwright's cause in the mid-1530's. All the more was this the case when Viceroy Antonio de Mendoza early was called upon to settle problems in New Galicia which stemmed largely from the continuing activities of the former president of the first audiencia, Nuño de Guzmán.

The presence of Cortés in New Spain at the time of the second López suit is a factor that can be interpreted variously. It might have expedited proceedings, or it might have constituted formidable opposition in realms of prestige, López' foe then bearing a title of nobility. Surely Cortés' absence in Spain at the time of the first case had not facilitated that court action.

Some matters related to López personally must have influenced the proceedings. His loss of fortune probably impaired his capacity to wage a long, costly court battle, even as it must have constituted an added incentive for the litigation of 1534. Nor could the witnesses called by López, simple workingmen, have helped at a time when the prestige factor was emerging strongly in the life of Mexico City and when officials fresh from Spain could hardly realize the shipbuilder's contribution.

As López' second flurry of litigation with Cortés died, the second audiencia was drawing to a close, soon to yield to an incoming viceroy. For many still-dissatisfied conquistadors it was a question of adjustment once more. Never did they surrender hope for reward, though they employed numerous methods to achieve their ends: some journeying to Spain, others appealing to the mother country from the New World, others persistently fighting for their rights on the soil of New Spain. Some acquired perpetual posts in the city council of Mexico City, others won coats of arms, and still others received profit-producing grants. López experienced none of this, but living as he did in a setting in which the conquistador class dominated more than half of the local posts—and had done so ever since the earliest days—he must have looked to the future uncertainly but hopefully as he heard of the approach of Viceroy Antonio de Mendoza.

In the short span of a decade Mexico City had learned how to welcome powerful personages. The good news of June, 1526, that Cortés was returning from Honduras—presumably from the dead—led to his being greeted with boundless hilarity and religious services of thanksgiving. A month later Luis Ponce, agent of royal will, received special private and public attention. In late 1528, when the first audiencia had landed on the coast, official greeters had gone out from Mexico City to meet the dignitaries. In January, 1531, every man in Mexico City who owned a horse had been required to sally forth to receive the judges of the second audiencia. Months later, when President Fuenleal arrived, trumpets, archways, and waiting throngs had greeted him. Now the time was at hand to greet a viceroy, the king's alter ego. Mexico City did him the honors shortly before mid-November, 1535.

# CHAPTER VIII

# SUBJECT OF THE FIRST VICEROY

EALTHY and highly respected as well as completely removed from the factional strife of New Spain, Mendoza, with his experience, his sense of justice, his humanity, his detachment, and his loyalty to the king, was an ideal choice for this first New World viceregal appointment. Of average height, his long head dominated by keen eyes and firm mouth, the bearded Mendoza had a commanding presence. Member of one of the ancient and influential families of Spain, he had repeatedly distinguished himself in service to crown and country. To give him official welcome, four councilmen of Mexico City, at least two of whom were veterans of the conquest, went forth to escort him into the city.[1]

While the viceroy employed the ensuing months to establish the pattern of his administration, conquistador López, like so many other citizens of the realm, went about the prosaic daily routines which suggested their patterns of life in Mexico City were already well rooted. In September, 1536, he was able to realize a pittance from the estate of Hernán Medel. Certain credits, representing minor debts owed Medel by more than a dozen individuals, were transferred by the heirs and executors of Medel to Martín López. One of the two men thus kindly disposed toward the former shipwright was his old neighbor of 1525, Francisco de Solís. López accepted the risk and responsibility of collecting somewhat more than 932 pesos from men who included kinsmen and former servants of Medel, blacksmiths and bridle makers, a broker, and a number of his own close friends. The latter included Andrés Núñez and Lázaro Guerrero.[2] What López actually realized from this transfer of credits cannot be determined, but it is not likely that he collected all.

The same month that found him grasping at this straw, López was busy helping someone who was less fortunate. At a moment when his own pocketbook was far from full, López, as cosigner for the debtor Juan Griego Girón, came forward with forty pesos in gold for the demanding creditor, Francisco Maldonado. Of course the former shipwright would have strained himself to escape humiliation at the hands of archenemy Maldonado, but equally important, in all likelihood, is the fact he was assisting a fellow conquistador who had served aboard a brigantine, who had been a colleague on the New Galicia campaign, and who had been his stanch witness in the court action of 1534.[3] Added proof of López' depressed financial status in this period is seen in the inclusion of his name on a lengthy list of debtors which the Segovian-born merchant Diego Espinar transferred to an agent for collection on November 29, 1536.[4]

Early 1537 produced another interesting episode in which

[1] Arthur Scott Aiton, *Antonio de Mendoza—First Viceroy of New Spain* (Durham, 1927), 14-15; *Actas de cabildo*, III, 3, 121, 123, 129.

[2] Millares Carlo and Mantecón, *Indice y extractos*, II, no. 1929.

[3] López, 1528-1574, pp. 114, 115, Conway Coll. (Aberdeen); Millares Carlo and Mantecón, II, no. 1903.

[4] Millares Carlo and Mantecón, II, no. 2073, with full text of document on pp. 264-78.

López figured. With the death of Pedro Álvarez, a seaman of Seville who had entered New Spain with the shipwright, Martín López became the guardian of his son Antón. López pursued the boy's interests by apprenticing him, on March 10, 1537, to silversmith Francisco Hernández for a five-year period. At the end of the interval, young Álvarez was to emerge a master craftsman, provided with the tools of the trade. Meanwhile, the lad would receive clothing, board, and room, as well as instruction, from silversmith Hernández.[5]

Martín López also was godfather to infant children of fellow residents of Mexico City. One such occasion came on a Sunday in mid-September, 1538, as Gonzalo de Moya and his wife Ana presented their infant son Lope for baptism in the cathedral in Mexico City, Martín López and his wife Juana serving as two of the four godparents of young Lope.[6] Nothing is known of the Moyas and their place in the life of Mexico City.

Once more López found it necessary, in 1537-1538, to continue the litigation with Maldonado. Under the viceroyalty, Maldonado in January of 1537 renewed the action against López for false imprisonment and ill treatment. López requested and received additional time to gather evidence from witnesses outside Mexico City, but on July 10, 1537, Maldonado requested the conclusion of the case; López expressed the same wish seven weeks later.

On April 5, 1538, the audiencia rendered its decision, against Martín López. From that moment on, López was to suffer perpetual deprivation of right to hold any post connected with the administration of justice. Only with express license could he ever occupy any such office in the future. Court costs were assessed against López.

Four days later, Maldonado's counsel appealed the decision because it did not include a monetary judgment against the condemned defendant. When López also protested the decision on April 9, the court designated a period for the initiation of appeal action. By the end of the month Maldonado's counsel had con-

---

[5] *Ibid.*, no. 2220.    [6] Libro 1° de bautisimos de la cathedral, fol. 24.

cluded the plaintiff's appeal. Two months later, on June 25, 1538, López answered the Maldonado appeal, closing with the request that the court revoke the existing sentence, and the proceedings entered another quiescent period in mid-1538.[7]

The shipwright who was singularly unsuccessful in his suits to obtain reward for his services during the conquest was remarkably successful when it came to obtaining honors which recognized those same services. In a twelve-year interval, no fewer than three different coats of arms were granted Martín López by the Spanish crown.

For approximately a quarter of a century of service in the New World, embracing the hazy days in Cuba as well as the years of soldiering, shipbuilding, and settlement in New Spain, López was granted a coat of arms on December 21, 1539. The shield pictured two brigantines afloat, with a closed helmet atop the shield.[8]

In this period in New Spain a coat of arms for oneself and family, often sought and often obtained, was a means of gaining social prestige. The crown surely was not unaware of the fact that the coats of arms, essentially an empty honor, represented a cheap form of remuneration for the conquistadors. One suspects that royal advisers often concluded that the awarding of coats of arms would help to wed conquistador loyalty to the crown.

However honored López felt when word arrived that he and his children could boast a coat of arms, he must have known that for a man whose name had been connected with such significant service it was indeed a very meager reward. The new honor was dated late in 1539, and the following year was rapidly slipping by before López knew of it.

As the year 1540 dawned, many adventurous souls of Mexico City and numerous other Spanish communities of New Spain were

[7] Maldonado contra López, I, 22-23; II, 4-5, 42, 67-116; III, 1-17, 98-99; IV, 41-56, Conway Coll. (Cambridge).

[8] Santiago Montoto, *Nobiliario hispano-americano del siglo xvi*, in Montoto and others, *Colección de documentos inéditos para la historia de Ibero-América* (14 vols., Madrid, 1927-1935), II, 212-15. The plates for the coats of arms of Martín López and Francisco Maldonado are reversed by Montoto, with López' incorrectly on page 229.

on the march, heading for a rendezvous far off to the northwest in Compostela, New Galicia. In response to the reports of Cabeza de Vaca and the quick reconnaissance of Friar Marcos of Nice, the lure of the far north had produced such a fever pitch of excitement that a mammoth expedition was being formed. To further this crown-endorsed project, Viceroy Mendoza named to its command the young governor of New Galicia, Francisco Vázquez de Coronado. On Sunday, February 22, 1540, Coronado mustered a force of 225 horsemen and 62 foot soldiers. Most of the men were nonconquistadors, younger men who sought new avenues to fame and fortune.[9] Indeed most of the surviving conquistadors, among them Martín López, were too old, too settled, too disillusioned, too occupied—even too civilian-minded—to respond to one more will-o'-the-wisp call of adventure. Now fifty years of age, with growing family responsibilities—and Juana was carrying the next child that February—one could hardly expect Martín López to dash around like every rosy-cheeked youth.

Two days after the military muster at Compostela, López was busy in Mexico City trying to help a veteran conquistador reconstruct an account of battles already fought and won. Diego Holguín, born of hidalgo strain in Cáceres, had come to New Spain just about the time of the fall of Tenochtitlán. His campaigning took place in Michoacán, Zacatula, Colima, and Jalisco. Nuño de Guzmán had stripped him of some of his holdings, and Cortés had seized most of the rest, reducing him to extreme poverty. Married and the father of a number of children, he found it impossible to live on the salary of 200 pesos received for administering a *corregimiento,* and so he appealed to the crown for recognition of his merits and more suitable reward for his services. Martín López, accustomed to calling upon his colleagues of days gone by in his own petitions and litigation, gave warmhearted support to Holguín's document.[10]

---

[9] Arthur S. Aiton (trans. and intro.), *The Muster Roll and Equipment of the Expedition of Francisco Vázquez de Coronado* (Ann Arbor, 1939).

[10] Información de los méritos y servicios de Diego Holguín (1540), Paso y Troncoso Coll., Leg. 95.

Having twice failed to achieve his ends through the judiciary,
López in 1540 petitioned the highest executive officers.[11] Aside
from the difference in governmental channels—and even in that
there was some repetition of personnel—López' presentation of
his cause was much the same. The plaintiff's complaint gave way
to a supplicant's petition, but the interrogatory of the courtroom
was still on hand, often almost verbatim in its phrasing in addition
to possessing the same general purposes. In court López had
hoped that the setting forth of his record of services would merit
monetary reward from Cortés; now he hoped that an account of
these services would win some royal grant. In 1540, as in 1528
and 1534, the conquistador sought honors and income. The shift
of López' focus from Cortés to crown must have been a reaction to
the realities of the moment. Cortés, in eclipse, departed from New
Spain early that year for the last time. The viceroyalty, apex of
royal power, had rooted itself deeply in five short years, so deeply
that Antonio de Mendoza was to be the first of a long line that
eventually included more than a half hundred viceroys for
New Spain.

In several respects the interrogatory presented by López in
1540 was a compromise between two earlier ones. With thirty
questions, it fell between the shorter one of 1528 and the longer
one of 1534. The great difference in 1540 lay in the witnesses.
Instead of long lists of men, López now called only a half-dozen
persons to lend support to his case. He continued to depend
wholly on conquistadors and still turned to some poor artisans,
but for the first time he also employed men of prominence on
the local political scene. Only one of them, Lázaro Guerrero, had
served previously as a López witness. Only one, again Guerrero,
had worked on the brigantines. Aside from the ubiquitous Lázaro
Guerrero, the witnesses of 1540—Bernardino Vázquez de Tapia,
Gerónimo Ruiz de la Mota, Antonio Bravo, Andrés de Tapia, and
Andrés de Trujillo—were different, perhaps significantly so.

------

[11] The record of this action is in López, 1529-1550, pp. 118-69, Conway
Coll. (LC).

As it came from the rich and the poor, the politically powerful and the politically insignificant, the well-born and the humble, from old friends and old enemies, this testimony of 1540 in behalf of Martín López was impressively consistent.

After the witnesses presented their testimony between May 20 and June 6, 1540, before Judge Montealegre, the member of the audiencia designated by Viceroy Mendoza to conduct the proceedings, the final record was presented to the viceroy, and the following undated viceregal opinion was signed by Antonio de Mendoza:

"To His Most Christian Majesty.

"Martín López, a resident of this city of Mexico, has submitted the enclosed enquiry into his services overseas with the request that after examining it I should forward it to your Majesty for your information. From its contents I gather that he served your Majesty well and faithfully in the capture of this city of Mexico and that it was due to his intelligence and industry that the brigantines were built which, under Providence, were one of the means by which this city was gained. He was afterwards granted the encomienda of a village hard by this city of but little worth. He is an honorable man, with a wife and children. He is worthy of whatever favor your Majesty may deem well to grant him."

The López petition of 1540 soon evoked royal reply, but passivity on the part of the viceroy is basic to any explanation of its very limited success. In the first place, Mendoza's moderate, matter-of-fact endorsement of the services of López suggests he was not unusually impressed. His failure to take direct personal action in the matter, and he could have done so, found Mendoza pursuing one of his most characteristic administrative techniques, that of doing little and doing that slowly.[12]

While Coronado was still trudging through the inhospitable northern country and Mendoza was facing the rebels of New Galicia, the unsuccessful litigant of 1528 and 1534 became a successful petitioner when his monarch replied from Talavera on

[12] Aiton, *Antonio de Mendoza,* 51-52.

May 24, 1541, to his document of 1540. Proof that the petition
had reached the royal ear is seen in the phrasing of the document
the crown sent to the viceroy. In it Spanish officials restated the
burden of the interrogatory in which López had related his
services. In so doing, the crown identified itself with a fuller and
warmer acceptance of the services of the shipwright than had been
extended by Viceroy Mendoza in New Spain. Having recognized
his services, the king proceeded to recommend Martín López, his
sons—especially his first-born—and their descendants for offices
and posts in the royal service in districts near their homes, as in
Cholula, Tlaxcala, Huejotzingo, Chalco, or Xochimilco. (In substance, this royal action of 1541 removed the officeholding dis-
ability levied upon Martín López in the audiencia decision of
1538.) The king additionally urged the viceroy to increase their
landholdings.[13] With transatlantic communication inordinately
slow and with a viceroy busy with more pressing business, it naturally would require time before royal recognition of his services
might be translated into improved well-being for Martín López.

Eighteen months after the royal recognition of López' services,
the viceroy decided to grant additional land to the supplicant.
Antonio de Mendoza on January 24, 1543, bestowed a ranching
establishment and two *caballerías* of land in the Tequixquiac
district upon him. A year later, on February 9, 1544, Mendoza
conferred upon López a site for an inn, as well as a half caballería
of land. The property lay within the limits of the pueblo of
Cuautitlán, about halfway between Mexico City and the conquistador's interests in Tequixquiac. Situated upon the road and
adjacent to the bridge spanning the river at Cuautitlán, it might
have been ideal for its designated purpose.[14] However, no record
is available regarding the use to which López put his property.
Since he remained a resident of Mexico City, it is quite likely
he leased it to some interested innkeeper.

[13] Porras Muñoz, "Martín López," in *Estudios Cortesianos*, 323-24.
[14] Mercedes, II, expediente 125; II, 279v (Archivo General de la Nación,
Mexico City).

Meanwhile, even the most important of petitions could not consume a man's every waking moment, and so it was that 1540 also found López repeatedly related to affairs taking place in the cathedral of Mexico City. When barber Francisco Gudiel's infant son was presented for baptism on May 13, Juana and Martín were two of the child's four godparents. With them was another conquistador and his wife, Pedro Valenciano, the cardplaying warrior who early in the conquest had reduced a leather drumhead to a crude deck of cards.[15]

Four months later, in early September, it was time for the baptism of the child that Martín's wife had been carrying at the moment of the muster of Coronado's force. As one suspects that Martín López was the social superior of little-known Gonzalo de Moya and barber Francisco Gudiel, so one also suspects he probably was beneath the station of the godparents of his son Agustín. However, the fact that military order commander Juan Infante and Gonzalo Cerezo accepted that responsibility suggests they were honored at the thought of being identified with López' family.[16]

Juan Infante was a person of some prominence from the moment of his arrival in New Spain after the fall of Tenochtitlán. In 1527-1528 he joined Fray Ramón Bernal in the establishment of a mining company. In one slave-purchasing transaction he was the partner of Diego Ramírez, longtime artisan friend of Martín López. Recipient of a coat of arms in late summer, 1538, he held, as encomendero, the productive districts of La Laguna until they were assigned to the crown. Subsequently, for many years, he held a number of encomiendas in the Bishopric of Michoacán. The second godfather in 1540 was Gonzalo Cerezo, a Narváez follower who had served as Cortés' page. On several postwar occasions he demonstrated leadership and concern as he sponsored appeals on economic and religious themes as well as on the

---

[15] Libro 1° de bautismos de la cathedral, fol. 56v; Millares Carlo and Mantecón, II, no. 1927; Díaz del Castillo, *Historia verdadera*, I, 413.
[16] Libro 1° de bautismos de la cathedral, fol. 63.

general rights of the conquistador class. Though his greatest service and prominence came only after midcentury as *alguacil mayor* of the audiencia of Mexico, a post the second marquis of the Valley of Oaxaca coveted for his half brother, he held, as encomendero, Socula in the Archbishopric of Mexico, an obviously rich grant with its annual income appraisal of 1,550 pesos.[17]

While one citizen of Mexico City was busy petitioning the crown, helping his friends to do likewise, having his own son baptized, and attending such services for the infant children of others—while one citizen of New Spain was immersed in the ways of civilian life, war clouds on the northern frontier had given way to bloodshed. The Mixton War, as the rebellion in New Galicia came to be termed, sprang from a complex of circumstances. Due to the unnecessary brutality which had stamped Nuño de Guzmán's conquest of that area a decade earlier, there existed more than the customary measure of ill will and suspicion between natives and Spaniards. The withdrawal of many of the latter as they took service in the ranks of Coronado's expedition afforded an opportunity for the smoldering hatred to come to the surface. All the more were the natives driven to use of force by the increasingly brutal treatment dealt out by the few Spaniards who remained in the region. Religion also took its place alongside the social, economic, and political complaints which inspired the fighting.

The Mixton War was the one great military challenge to royal authority during the term of Viceroy Mendoza, and as such, it permitted that official to demonstrate his military aptitude. Like the Coronado expedition, it drew the attention of a small number of the oldtime conquistadors, among them Diego Hernández

17 *Actas de cabildo,* I, 97; Millares Carlo and Mantecón, I, nos. 357, 531, 532, 533, 928, 1703; Pacheco and others, *Colección de documentos inéditos,* XXVI, 218-19, 505; XXVIII, 317; Ignacio de Villar Villamil (ed.), *Cedulario heráldico de conquistadores de Nueva España* (Mexico City, 1933), no. 61; Paso y Troncoso, *Epistolario de Nueva España,* IV, 149; VII, 282; IX, 10, 13; X, 12, 56; XIV, 148, 152; XV, 95-96; González de Cossío, *El libro de las tasaciones,* 143-44; López, 1529-1550, pp. 107-10, Conway Coll. (LC).

Nieto, Antonio de Oliver, and Gregorio de Villalobos. Cortés' onetime page, Gonzalo Cerezo, now risen to prominence, was another original conquistador in the ranks of the viceroy as he set forth to put down the rebellion in Jalisco. The holder of one of the earliest encomiendas granted by Cortés, dated April 4, 1522, Cerezo had established a household which, by the early 1540's, included a widowed sister and her children and grandchildren. As alguacil mayor of the viceregal court he might have felt real compulsion to accompany the viceroy on this military campaign. Most prominent of that older fighting force now destined for duty in Jalisco was Pedro de Alvarado, the last survivor of the trio of courageous captains who had campaigned at the side of Cortés. Indeed, the Mixton War closed out his colorful career, for he lost his life in a battlefield accident during an unsuccessful assault upon the fortress of Nochistlán.[18]

Peace did not return to New Galicia until 1542, the year which also marked the return of Coronado's longsuffering and disillusioned expeditionary force. The shipwright-hidalgo, who had not identified himself with Coronado's expedition, also stayed at home when Mendoza's force went off to the Mixton War. Martín López was not a party to the disappointment of Coronado, nor did he witness the success of Mendoza on the battlefield. Now well into his fifties, his contributions to the Hispanization of New Spain were reserved for less strenuous projects.

In early 1541 an ordinance expelling vagrants and gamblers from Mexico City was passed by the cabildo. Two of the four councilmen present were early conquistadors, Ruy González and Antonio de Carvajal. The latter had come to the Indies as a brash youth of eighteen, almost full thirty years earlier. Now forty-six years old, father of an infant son, and a long-term participant in the public affairs of New Spain in general and Mexico City in par-

---

[18] Información de los méritos y servicios de Juan Freyle (1544), Paso y Troncoso Coll., Leg. 94; Información de Gregorio de Villalobos (1554), *ibid.*, Leg. 97; Información de los méritos y servicios de Gonzalo Cerezo (1543), *ibid.*, Leg. 93; Aiton, *Antonio de Mendoza*, 137-58.

ticular, he epitomized the positive contributions of the conquistador turned settler. The day following passage of this ordinance it was duly proclaimed in public by the town crier. In the plaza on February 9, as Arguyjo raised his voice to announce the action, was Martín López, whose name, along with several others, went into the municipal record as witness.[19]

A year later, on February 16, 1542, López testified in support of the statement of services presented by fellow conquistador, brigantine-builder, and crewman Lázaro Guerrero, who in turn had testified in favor of the shipwright in 1528, 1534, and 1540.[20]

Three months later to the day, on May 16, 1542, López joined a distinguished throng testifying in behalf of the services of the deceased Indian woman interpreter, the well-remembered Marina. In company with Gerónimo López, Francisco de Santa Cruz, Francisco de Terrazas, Gerónimo Ruiz de la Mota, Leonel de Cervantes, Bernardino Vázquez de Tapia, and Antonio de Carvajal, more than one of whom had been his enemy under other circumstances and all of whom were prominent in the life of Mexico City, López extolled the woman whose labors had been indispensable to the early conquistador successes.[21]

While several of the above events were in the making, flurries of the indecisive litigation between López and Maldonado also became matters of record in 1539. The last discernible, though distinctly not the final, phase of the tangled Maldonado-Cortés-López court controversy appeared in 1540 and 1541. Over the signatures of lawyers Ceynos, Loaisa, and Tejada, on March 20, 1540, a two-point decision was handed down in favor of Cortés. Having proved his case to the satisfaction of the audiencia, Cortés was awarded eighty gold bars, each valued at seven pesos. This was the type of bar the natives of the Tehuantepec region were accustomed to presenting in payment of tribute. Within nine

[19] *Actas de cabildo*, IV, 228-29; Información de los méritos y servicios de Ruy González (1558), Paso y Troncoso Coll., Leg. 94; Gardiner, *Naval Power*, 136, 208.

[20] Información de los méritos y servicios de Lázaro Guerrero (1542), Paso y Troncoso Coll., Leg. 94.

[21] Pacheco and others, XLI, 213-14, 226-28.

days López was due to pay this sum as the amount of tribute in arrears and due Cortés at the time López entered upon his duties as alcalde mayor of Tehuantepec. A vaguely phrased second part of the decision stated that López would be required to pay the marquis a sum yet to be determined as damages for having removed the pueblo of Xalapa from the control of Cortés.

A year later, López' counsel was pursuing an appeal which had carried the issue to Spain and the Council of the Indies. Even as he did so, lawyer Vicencio de Riberol urged that the appeal be forwarded without the defendant's posting the usual surety because Martín López was bonded for the amount involved in the award and also because he held property worth considerably more than that sum. (The latter statement, although jolting to the almost perennial plea of López that he was well-nigh penniless, does not contradict it. López never denied he held property but rather insisted it produced an inadequate income for him and his family.) A last glimpse of this revealing yet unproductive litigation is dated April 1, 1541, at which moment it was still in its appeal status before the Council of the Indies.[22]

While Coronado struggled against nature in the far north, Mendoza fought rebels in New Galicia, and López battled Maldonado in the courts of Mexico City, a matter was brewing in the mother country which soon put most of the Spaniards in New Spain in a belligerent mood. In Spain advising the Council of the Indies on Indian matters, the famous defender of the natives, Las Casas, was penning and publicizing the contents of his "Brevissima relación de la destruyción de las Indias," a work which condemned conquistador handling of the natives. A direct product of Las Casas' agitation, the New Laws of 1542 held that enslaved Indians should be freed and no more could be enslaved, that encomenderos with excessive numbers of Indians should surrender some of them, that no encomienda could be inherited by the heirs of the present holder, and that church and govern-

---

[22] Maldonado contra López, IV, 57-91, Conway Coll. (Cambridge); Hospital de Jesús, 300/107.

ment officials should surrender their Indians immediately. This was a momentous blow to the way of life of the average Spaniard in New Spain, conquistador and latecomer alike.

Restlessness and complaint greeted the arrival of the laws in New Spain in late 1543. Literate and able Gerónimo López, who frequently resorted to pen to put his personal complaints before the throne, wrote the king that the new legislation would be the cause of the destruction and loss of New Spain. Fellow conquistador Francisco de Terrazas, not content with attacking the new order, insisted that the conquistadors deserved perpetual encomiendas. Buttressing the complaint of the individual went the protest of the cabildo of Mexico City and that of the audiencia of New Spain.[23] Indignant and belligerent, the citizens of New Spain tempered their restlessness with the hope that the crown would either stay the execution of the laws or see fit to cancel them entirely. Meanwhile, the very men who had just deflated the explosive potential of the Mixton War were themselves representatives of a new unrest.

On the viceregal plane the New Laws had scarcely seized the focus of attention from the late Mixton War when they, in turn, knew competition from *Visitador* Francisco Tello de Sandoval. Possessed of wide powers, he was authorized to investigate royal administration from Viceroy Mendoza down to the lowest officer of the smallest town in New Spain. Arriving in New Spain early in 1544, the visitador spent the next four years in that land. For two years in the middle forties the royal agent who made every other official feel ill at ease listened to complaints and piled up the evidence out of which formal charges might ultimately evolve. Those were days when disgruntled citizens poured their streams of complaint into the ear of the willing listener. However, Viceroy Mendoza ably defended himself against the forty-four accusations Tello de Sandoval leveled at him, and so he continued as the king's highest officer in the land. Not least of his acts, before his

---

[23] Aiton, *Antonio de Mendoza,* 95-96; Paso y Troncoso, IV, 60-61, 64-75, 102-14.

departure from New Spain, had been Tello de Sandoval's suspension of those sections of the New Laws which hit the encomenderos hardest—suspended long enough at least for them to take their case to Spain in person.[24]

López' relationship to all this can be surmised, though no details are available. As an encomendero and father, he surely wanted to keep what he held and eventually pass it on to his eldest son. Accordingly, he might have been among the disgruntled citizens of Mexico City who threatened to greet the arriving visitador in mourning garb until the viceroy dissuaded them from such a biting demonstration of their point of view. López might have been one who went to the visitador with complaint against the existing administration. He might have been one who helped to organize and finance the sending of procurators to Spain to set forth the case for continuance of encomiendas. Though the record is silent, commonsense would indicate such actions as plausible from a man who, with lots of fighting spirit and little property, traditionally had fought in behalf of his own self-interest.

Martín López on July 1, 1544, petitioned the throne for a specified income. Complaining of his impoverished condition, large family, advancing age, and meager income from his encomienda, he requested that "from your Royal Treasury or from the Indian tributes paid to the Crown, I be given one thousand pesos per year for the maintenance of my children and household. . . . I have endured my poverty with fortitude awaiting the general allotment of territories which for a long time past your Highness, we have been told, has had in contemplation, for the compensation of the poorer conquistadors who are maintaining themselves with such difficulty, but now my circumstances force me to appeal to your Highness."[25]

López had certified copies of the interrogatories and testimony of 1528 and 1534 accompany the petition of 1544 to Spain. Once

---

[24] Aiton, *Antonio de Mendoza*, 97, 161-70.
[25] López, 1528-1574, pp. 1-2, Conway Coll. (Aberdeen).

more official delays were faced in New Spain, for the transcript requested in 1544 was not in his hands until 1547. It was this action of 1544-1547 which unified the records of the two cases within the single source cited by the present writer. Viceroy Mendoza limited himself to another lukewarm endorsement of López.[26] Perhaps the appeal of 1544, along with the block of transcribed earlier records, did eventually influence the issuance of royal cedulas in 1550.

On June 18, 1547, López and his wife were presenting son Bernabé for baptism. In the choice of Tristán de Luna y Arellano and *Factor* Hernando de Salazar as godparents for their child, Martín and Juana again demonstrated their relations with rich and powerful segments of the community.[27]

As an officer with Coronado in the late 1530's and early 1540's, as leader of a Mendoza-inspired punitive campaign against insurgent Indians in 1548, as a friend of Viceroys Mendoza and Velasco and the Cortés family, don Tristán de Luna y Arellano was one of the great names of the period. This holder of numerous high offices in New Spain, having married the wealthy widow of Francisco Maldonado, the foe of Alcalde Mayor Martín López in 1529 and for years thereafter, held in encomienda various pueblos in Oaxaca, among them Mitla, Achutla, Atoyaque, and Chicomeaguatepeque. A decade later, Tristán de Luna y Arellano led an expedition to the coast of Florida.[28]

The second godfather honoring López' son in 1547 was Factor Hernando de Salazar. Son of royal Factor Gonzalo de Salazar, who arrived in New Spain in the early 1520's and remained a power in government, including long service in the cabildo, until his death at midcentury, Hernando was a particularly prominent personage between 1543 and his death late in 1550. For more than two years (1542-1544), he served as councilman of Mexico

26 *Ibid.*, 143-44.
27 Libro 1° de bautisimos de la cathedral, fols. 151v, 185, 187.
28 González de Cossío, xiii, 13-15, 87, 174, 248; Paso y Troncoso, VIII, 257; Pacheco and others, III, 365; IV, 136; XIII, 264; XIV, 318, 321, 326; XV, 98, 376; Aiton, *Antonio de Mendoza*, 175.

City, but his most important service was as factor for the half-dozen years preceding his death.[29]

When the church contacts are added to the people known by López the litigant, the encomendero, the petitioner, and the witness in support of the cases of others, it is evident that Martín López was widely known among the Spaniards of Mexico City.

The untiring López in the late 1540's petitioned that either he or one of his sons be allowed to sit in the enclosure reserved for lawyers during the hearing of suits, buttressing his request with certificates which testified to his hidalgo origin. Whether this privilege he sought was psychological and social or a preliminary to essaying the role of his own attorney is unknown. López did, however, stress the fact that even then he had suits pending against Hernán Medel and Hernando Cortés. The audiencia of Mexico complied with his request, on December 22, 1548, and granted the conquistador, or his eldest son, permission to sit in the reserved section of the courtroom.[30]

On May 15, 1550, in the twilighttime of the administration of Viceroy Mendoza in New Spain, royal word went out from the mother country that Martín López was accorded a second coat of arms. This time a vertical line divided the shield into two equal sections. Two golden galleys on white and blue waters commemorated the industry of the shipwright who had built the much-needed thirteen brigantines. The second half of the shield showed a naked sword outlined in gold and hanging point down against a field of red. The significance of the sword was not stated in the text of the grant, but obviously represented the general soldierly services of the conquistador, which Bernal Díaz had in mind as he termed Martín López "a good soldier in all the wars."[31]

With a border of stars and crosses the elaborate second shield, like the livestock brand of the 1520's, hinted at López' religious nature. Fringing the two ships were four golden Jerusalem

[29] *Actas de cabildo,* IV, 312–V, 76 *passim;* Paso y Troncoso, IV, 52-53, 84, 195; V, 98, 103, 193; VI, 4, 45, 51-52, 142; VIII, 260; XV, 19.
[30] López, 1529-1550, pp. 173-74, Conway Coll. (LC).
[31] Díaz del Castillo, *The True History,* II, 300.

crosses on a field of red, and bordering the half picturing the
sword were four eight-pointed golden stars on a field of blue. As
in 1539, a closed helmet rested atop the colorful shield. Above the
helmet, and new to the device of 1550, was a black eagle bearing
a green standard on which appeared one Jesusalem cross. As with
the sword, no part of the text of the grant explained the eagle
and standard.[32]

Three weeks later, on June 7, 1550, two more cedulas recom-
mending Martín López and his family were penned by royal
officials in Valladolid, again in reply to a petition from the aging
conquistador. This time the viceroys and audiencias of the New
World were instructed to give Martín López special consideration
as a potential *corregidor*. With daughters approaching marriageable age, López must have been additionally happy to have the
king state that the men who married them would receive special
consideration for royal posts.[33] Nonetheless, it remained for the
second viceroy to appoint López to such a position. With only
one of his five daughters married by 1560 (by then all were old
enough for matrimony) one doubts the importance of the royal
promise regarding posts for their future husbands.

One year after the second coat of arms had been conferred upon
López, a third one was granted him from Madrid on May 20,
1551. With but minor pictorial variations from the second coat
of arms, this final form taken by the arms of Martín López is
noteworthy for the fuller textual explanation of the elements
composing it. Replacing the fringe of crosses and stars on the
shield of 1550 were lions representing seven provinces in which
López had served his king. The remainder was substantially
the same.[34]

As conquistador petitioners related on paper their services to
the crown, so, too, royal reward was often reduced to paper, the
piece which granted a weary old warrior a coat of arms. Martín

[32] La Sociedad de Bibliófilos Españoles, *Nobiliario de conquistadores de Indias*
(Madrid, 1892), 193-94. The López coat of arms is item three on plate 41.
[33] Porras Muñoz, in *Estudios Cortesianos*, 324-25.
[34] *Ibid.*, 325-26.

López was one whose repeated requests for payment in gold pesos were repeatedly countered by high-sounding concessions on sheets of paper bearing the royal seal.

Even as the growing number of mouths to feed complicated an already difficult economic situation for Martín and Juana López, the pride and persistence of the parents did help to produce and maintain a happy, hospitable, though humble household. Even while in reduced circumstances, López continued to succor the less fortunate. Juan Griego Girón declared in 1560 that "ever since he had known Martín López, which was for more than fifty years, he had seen that he was very open-handed and charitable, always ready to help the poor and the needy."[35]

With the man who never had enough for himself always possessing sufficient to share with others, all is relative concerning Martín López' economic position in this period. Persistently the importunate petitioner, he might have been thought penniless; endlessly generous and living at a social level that called for means, he must have possessed some wealth.

Of middle age when Mendoza came to New Spain, López was an old man before the departure of the first viceroy. Never in all that interval was he the object of more than the most modest measure of viceregal or royal consideration. Uncertain as he witnessed his arrival, López possibly viewed the withdrawal of Antonio de Mendoza from New Spain without great regret.

[35] López, 1528-1574, pp. 153, 186, Conway Coll. (Aberdeen).

# CHAPTER IX

# LATE IN LIFE AND PAST MIDCENTURY

THE SECOND viceroy of New Spain, Luis de Velasco, was another appointee of noble origins, long military service, distinguished administrative experience, and fine personal qualities. Met by Mendoza at Cholula, he was escorted by him into Mexico City late in 1550. His conscientious predecessor, before withdrawing to the Pacific coast to take ship for his own new post in Peru, briefed him on the problems he faced in New Spain.

The year 1550 found New Spain in the midst of many things. A successor to the first archbishop, now several years in his grave, was about to assume his responsibilities. Many conquistadors were dead. Recently laid to rest in an Old World grave, Cortés had outlived his trio of great captains, Alvarado, Sandoval, and Olid. And with the passing of such great names, it is mistakenly assumed the conquistador element had passed from the scene. But many veterans unknown in the 1520's had become prominent in New Spain by 1550.

Guatemala City, point of final settlement for many of the men who had followed Pedro de Alvarado into Central America, counted numerous early conquistadors among its citizens. There lived Bernal Díaz del Castillo, the foot soldier who in later years immortalized himself and his colleagues by his classic account of the conquest of New Spain; Pedro González Nájera, who had served aboard a brigantine during the siege of Tenochtitlán; Pedro de Ovide, an obscure follower of Narváez in 1520 who by 1551 had risen to the post of alcalde ordinario of Guatemala; and Andrés de Rodas, Hernando de Illescas, Cristóbal Rodríguez Picón, Cristóbal de Salvatierra, Francisco Sánchez, and Juan Fernández Nájera, among others.[1]

In Puebla, more commonly called Los Angeles in mid-sixteenth-century years, some of the thirty-four conquistador founders of the municipality two decades earlier were not only present but still active in community life. By midcentury many of the conquistadors who had helped to found Puebla—among them Alonso Galeote, Pedro de Villanueva, Martín de Calahorra, and Francisco de Oliveros—had so identified themselves with that Spanish community as to guarantee it successful growth and a permanent place among the settlements of New Spain.[2]

Even storm-tossed, disease-ridden Vera Cruz possessed enough appeal to cause an occasional old conquistador, like Pedro Moreno, to fix his residence in the principal port of the colony. Like the east coast, the Pacific slope still was home at midcentury to early conquistadors such as Seville-born Juan Fernández.[3]

---

[1] Información de los méritos y servicios de Juan de Aragón (1551), Paso y Troncoso Coll., Leg. 93; Información de los méritos y servicios de Juan Fernández Nájera (1551), *ibid.*, Leg. 94; Información de los méritos y servicios de Francisco Sánchez (1551), *ibid.*, Leg. 97.

[2] Información de los méritos y servicios de Alonso Ortiz de Zúñiga (1553), *ibid.*, Leg. 96; Información de Pedro de Villanueva (1554), *ibid.*, Leg. 97; Paso y Troncoso, *Epistolario de Nueva España*, III, 138; IX, 11, 23.

[3] Información de los méritos y servicios de Pedro Moreno (1553), Paso y Troncoso Coll., Leg. 95; Información de los méritos y servicios de Juan Fernández (1536, 1558, 1561, 1572), *ibid.*, Leg. 94.

Spread though they were through the length and breadth of the land, the conquistadors had an easily understood preference for Mexico City, at once both the fountainhead of change and the reservoir of the status quo. Here conquistadors quietly but nonetheless vigorously skirmished continuously against viceregal and archiepiscopal programs intended to further royal will at the expense, in varying degrees, of conquistador interests. Here they battled to hold what they had, even as they petitioned for more.

In 1550 conquistadors constituted an important element in the official life of the major municipality of New Spain. One of the two alcaldes ordinarios was Andrés de Tapia; and three of the lifetime councilmen—likewise senior members in point of service—were the veterans Bernardino Vázquez de Tapia, Antonio de Carvajal, and Ruy González.[4]

Outside the cabildo at midcentury in Mexico City the conquistador element could be found at every level of life: witness proud and wealthy Martín de Ircio, husband to María de Mendoza, sister of Viceroy Antonio de Mendoza; impoverished Diego Hernández Nieto, a bastard son of Seville; and much-married Alonso Ortiz de Zúñiga, whose offspring were about as numerous as his petitions and court actions.[5]

At the midpoint of the sixteenth century on the rich, sprawling mainland between the Gulf and the Pacific the conquistador class was still a significant factor, both quantitatively and qualitatively, in the multifacet life of New Spain.

To the shipwright of the conquest, a man with pride and fighting spirit that knew no diminution with advancing age, midcentury, with a new viceroy and a new archbishop, brought a revival of hopes for remuneration for signal services, a salaried post for himself in the royal service, opportunities for his eldest son, income that would provide dowries for daughters, comforts for himself and his wife in their declining years.

[4] *Actas de cabildo,* I-V *passim.*
[5] Aiton, *Antonio de Mendoza,* 10-11, 167; Información de los méritos y servicios de Diego Hernández Nieto (1539), Paso y Troncoso Coll., Leg. 95; Información de Alonso Ortiz de Zúñiga (1553), *ibid.,* Leg. 96; Paso y Troncoso, IX, 22.

Shortly before the death in 1548 of Zumárraga, the diocese of Mexico had been raised to an archdiocese, but it was 1551 before Archbishop Alonso de Montúfar entered upon the duties destined to occupy him for more than twenty years. With Montúfar and Velasco facing the future with energy and ability, it was a moment, in the early 1550's, of hope for all New Spain.

But Martín López had more than just a new administration on which to base his hopes. A royal cedula emanating from Madrid on November 10, 1551, possessed more significance for the conquistador than all the previous recommendations accorded him by the crown. Addressing him as Martín López Ossorio, his king identified the conquistador with the powerful branch of the family in the peninsula. Hailed as a man of valor and rare virtues, his name was specifically associated with the direct lineage of the illustrious Pedro Álvarez Ossorio. The throne remembered his part in the conquest: "among your brave deeds was the building of thirteen brigantines . . . which were the principal means of winning the city of Mexico." After references to his other services and to his losses and poverty, the crown restated the honors conferred upon him with the coat of arms of 1551, adding that López was to enjoy all the rights and prerogatives of a caballero. The recommendation of 1541, giving priority of consideration for himself and his descendants as potential officeholders, was reiterated. Henceforth the hidalgo shipwright was privileged to appear and seat himself at the public sessions of the authorities of any city or town. If he moved into newly populated communities, López was to be awarded double the normal grants of land and building sites. He was permitted an escort of up to four sword-bearing Negroes wherever he might go in the royal realms. The royal concession stated that these privileges were to be enjoyed perpetually by the direct male descendants of Martín López.[6]

This royal recommendation evoked almost immediate response from the second viceroy. Neither López nor Velasco could long have known of the king's latest endorsement of the conquistador

[6] Porras Muñoz, "Martín López," in *Estudios Cortesianos,* 326-29.

when the viceroy bestowed a land grant upon the former shipwright. On June 21, 1552, a sheep-ranching site within the limits
of the pueblo of Xilotepeque was given to Martín López. The
ranch next to his was held by the former brigantine captain who
lived across the street from him in Mexico City, Gerónimo Ruiz
de la Mota.[7] Coming as it did so early in the viceregal term of
Luis de Velasco, the grant must have convinced López that better
days were ahead.

Prior to the issuance of López' grant the Indians of the Xilotepeque region had complained repeatedly of the depredations
of Spanish-owned animals. By the time the shipwright came to
be identified with the area, this problem had the attention of
Visitador Diego Ramírez. During a visita that found many conquistadors condemned by the royal investigator, Martín López
drew no criticism from that royal agent, possibly because his ranch
was so small it did not attract the attention of the busy investigator, or possibly because Ramírez' death might have forestalled
a visit to López' holding.[8]

The Xilotepeque property quite possibly led to a contact
which might have paved the way for viceregal consideration of
Martín López' petitions for a royal post. The most powerful and
wealthy encomendero in the Xilotepeque district was none other
than Francisco de Velasco, brother of Viceroy Luis de Velasco.
Married to Beatriz de Andrada, daughter of conquistador Leonel
de Cervantes, Francisco de Velasco held one-half of Xilotepeque
in encomienda, the richest single grant listed in the survey of
1560. That year the encomienda of Xilotepeque, the other half
of which was held by Luis de Quesada, produced an annual
income of 17,000 pesos in cash and goods. After the death of his
brother, the viceroy, Francisco de Velasco served the interests of
the crown as captain general charged with putting down the rebellious conspirators of the mid-1560's. For his services on that
occasion he was designated a councilman of Mexico City by King

[7] Gregorio López, "Chronica de Nueva España en el años 1552-1553," fols.
65v-66, in E. E. Ayer Collection (Newberry Library).
[8] Walter V. Scholes, *The Diego Ramírez Visita* (Columbia, Mo., 1946).

The López Arms, May 15, 1550

Philip on May 10, 1567, a responsibility he assumed in early November of the same year and continued to exercise for years thereafter. Although Francisco de Velasco originally might have been but an entree to his more important brother, Viceroy Luis de Velasco, he was himself a powerful figure in Mexico City for years after his brother's death in 1564. Thus any contact López might have had with him, supplementing his direct appeals to the crown in Spain and the viceroy and the audiencia in New Spain, could have been doubly significant over a period of two decades.[9]

Efforts of the dead Zumárraga and the departed Mendoza bore fruit with the establishment in Mexico City of the first university on the continent of North America, the royal permission of September, 1551, being followed by the registration of the first students in June of 1553. Francisco Cervantes de Salazar, noted Spanish humanist come to lecture in the new university, composed for his students a dialogue on "The Interior of the City of Mexico" in 1554. In it the conversation-description of the city and its recent history led the outsider to inquire how it happened that Cortés was able to win his great victory in a setting unfit for cavalry or infantry. One of his guide-informants replied: "He out-did their skill with his skill. First having determined the depth of the water, with the aid of Martín López, he constructed small boats."[10] This was the first published work to honor the shipwright of the conquest by name. Possibly Martín López was unaware that his name had been recorded for posterity, for after all, in the Latin text of Cervantes de Salazar it was rendered Martini Lupi.[11]

The quality of the clergy of New Spain, which might in time be one of the numerous aspects of life influenced by the young university, drew the continuous attention of Archbishop Montúfar.

[9] Paso y Troncoso, VIII, 28; IX, 30; X, 198-99, 202, 217-18, 232; Juan Suárez de Peralta, *Noticias históricas de la Nueva España*, ed. by Justo Zaragoza (Madrid, 1878), 208-209, 220; *Actas de cabildo*, VII, 370-71ff.
[10] Francisco Cervantes de Salazar, *Life in the Imperial and Loyal City of Mexico in New Spain and the Royal and Pontifical University of Mexico*, trans. by Minnie Lee Barrett, ed. by Carlos Eduardo Castañeda (Austin, 1953), 47.
[11] *Ibid.*, fol. 265r.

Try as he might to translate ideal clerical standards into reality, that conscientious churchman faced an insurmountable task as long as he was hindered by a severe shortage of personnel.

Many conquistadors dedicated children to the service of the church. By the mid-1550's Andrés de Tapia's third son and Graviel de Villalobos, son of conquistador Gregorio de Villalobos, were active clergymen in New Spain. Indeed, occasional veterans did not thrust the task entirely into the hands of the next generation but often meaningfully identified themselves with religious endeavors: witness the example of Francisco Morante, who took the habit of the Order of St. Francis.[12] Beyond regularized marriages for themselves and Christian baptism for their offspring, many others diligently provided the natives entrusted to them with religious instruction. Some built chapels; others established lay brotherhoods dedicated to humanitarian works.

Sometime in 1556 Velasco further honored the royal cedulas of recommendation of 1541 and 1551 by appointing Martín López as corregidor of Tlasco. In the absence of conclusive proof, it can only be assumed that the Tlasco in which López served was the community so named in the northernmost part of the present state of Puebla, very close to the Hidalgo state line. In the mountains of the Sierra Madre Oriental and close to their eastern slope, Tlasco lay slightly more than 100 miles by air to the northeast of Mexico City and some 40-50 miles due west of Papantla. Such a remote physical setting, in a marginal mining zone removed from the centers of Spanish activity, combined with a meager salary, suggests Martín López was far from being the recipient of a choice post as corregidor of Tlasco. His willingness to go into such primitive country is additional evidence of his financial need in the mid-1550's.

Of the conquistador's service in that office little is known except that with the expiration of the normal three-year tour of duty his satisfactory record led the viceroy to extend his term

---

[12] Información de los méritos y servicios de Francisco Morante (1551), Paso y Troncoso Coll., Leg. 95; Información de Gregorio de Villalobos (1554), *ibid.*, Leg. 97; Paso y Troncoso, VII, 183-84, 293.

on September 18, 1559, for an additional sixteen months. In the document granting this extension of office, Viceroy Velasco said he was motivated by the excellence of López' services and "by other causes," which he did not enumerate. Although a corregidor's income was seldom, if ever, synonymous with the official salary paid him, it is noteworthy that López was to receive but 200 pesos for the additional period of service, a sum which provides some insight into what must have been his salary for the other three years.[13] If, as this figure suggests, Corregidor López received an official income of approximately 150 pesos annually, his post must have been a very ordinary appointment. In the Compostela district of New Galicia for the year of 1562, for instance, eleven corregidores averaged 146 pesos each, while in the Guadalajara district of the same province, the annual average for fifteen such officials was 176 pesos.[14]

During this period when López was in his late sixties and early seventies, little information is available. The willingness of the viceroy to extend his term as corregidor suggests that he was capable.

Before his extended term as corregidor expired, Martín López appeared, on April 20, 1560, before the audiencia to request certain affidavits testifying to his lineage, rank, services, children, and poverty to support his petition for another government post for himself and consideration for his children. The former shipwright presented an eighteen-question interrogatory with the request that seven designated witnesses be called to testify on the matters treated therein. With the passing of twenty years and the winning of modest honors and posts, both the interrogatory and the witnesses differed from the appeal of 1540.[15]

This time López concentrated on nonmilitary aspects of his career. In fact, for the first time he said nothing about his services during the 1519-1521 interval. Because he wanted to be con-

---

[13] Porras Muñoz, in *Estudios Cortesianos*, 329.
[14] Paso y Troncoso, IX, 196-204.
[15] The record of this petition is found in López, 1528-1574, pp. 147-86, Conway Coll. (Aberdeen).

sidered for significant royal posts, he established his relationship
to the proud, tax-exempt, armorial hidalgo strain of Andalusia.
Because he was justifiably proud of his service as alcalde mayor in
Tehuantepec and as corregidor in Tlasco, he stressed his administrative contributions to good government in New Spain. Because
he was poor, he discussed his encomienda at Tequixquiac, the
unmarried daughters in seclusion at home, the sons that could not
be maintained and educated in Mexico City and who accordingly
were in service in remote parts of the colony. Special attention
was called to his first-born son, who needed a post. Short though
it was, the interrogatory cleverly explored the political, economic,
and social sides of four decades of López' life in New Spain in
addition to his Spanish origins.

Meanwhile, the López household of 1560 was far from attractive.
It was one thing for the conquistador to refer to the "impoverished and necessitous situation" which found him "penniless and
crippled with debts," and something else for him to expand such
verbal generalities into the specific hardships he and his family
faced. As a man of quality, he had been accustomed to maintaining regularly in his household men at arms and horses, but
with the 1550's he was no longer able to afford such an establishment. Indeed, so excessive was his indebtedness it exceeded the
total value of his estate. Not only had the luxuries of the hidalgo's
way of life disappeared, but the López household was reduced to
the level of bare subsistence. Unable to sustain all of his offspring
at home, López sent three sons away from Mexico City because
he could not provide for the educations they needed; one was in
Guatemala, another in Oaxaca, and the third in New Galicia.
Ashamed of the poverty that denied his sons the normal advan-
tages enjoyed by male descendants of hidalgos, Martín López
disrupted his family and sent some members far afield, where the
social standards were not so financially exacting for caballeros.
The pain caused by such a rupture of the unity of his family is
evident in López' plea for "a decent and reasonable estate and
income" which would permit the maintenance of all his family
in Mexico City.

The numerous López girls joined their brothers in feeling the pinch of the family's financial straits. Four of the five daughters, still unmarried, were quietly living in the seclusion of their home in 1560 because their hidalgo father lacked the means to provide suitable dowries for them. Witnesses grieved that such honorable and modest young ladies were thus denied merited opportunities at marriage. The López household faced a dilemma common to New Spain, for the problem of dowries for daughters had drawn official attention repeatedly.

With the passing of years and the marked stratification of colonial society, the question of the dowry had become a paramount issue in New Spain. Even the cabildo cried out against practices through which great numbers of fine young ladies were denied marriage because of the financial demands of the dowry and the prevailing styles of expensive dress. Nor did the too common tendency on the part of young men of means to go to Spain for their wives improve the unhappy lot of the maids of Mexico.[16] Girls denied matrimony under such artificial circumstances turned in great numbers to the church, swelling the female religious communities of New Spain.

Meanwhile, a dowry had been provided for Juana, and the eldest López girl became the bride of Francisco Pérez del Castillo. The obscurity attending his name suggests that no particularly powerful tie had been established thereby. The best index to the position of Francisco and Juana in the community is seen in the eventual marriage of their son Luis to a granddaughter of Gerónimo Ruiz de la Mota, fellow conquistador who lived across the street from Martín López.[17]

The poverty of Martín López and his family in 1560 stemmed, in part, from the small income he obtained from the encomienda embracing half of the pueblo of Tequixquiac. In a day of in-

---

[16] *Actas de cabildo*, VII, 59, 63-66.

[17] Edmundo O'Gorman, "Catálogo de pobladores de Nueva España," *Boletín del Archivo General de la Nación*, XIII (1942), 140; Baltasar Dorantes de Carranza, *Sumaria relación de las cosas de la Nueva España, con noticia individual de los descendientes legítimos de los conquistadores, y primeros pobladores españoles* (Mexico City, 1902), 215-16.

flated prices and debased pesos, the encomendero was receiving
four hundred pesos annual income from his encomienda. The
Tequixquiac area was cold, the soil was poor, and most years
the crops were frostbitten. Witness after witness asserted that in
view of the rising level of prices and the peculiar needs López
faced as he tried to launch sons and daughters into adult life, he
would have had barely enough if his encomienda had produced
ten times as much as it actually did.[18]

Nor was it enough simply to detail past record and present
circumstance in a petition in 1560; one also must hint at hoped-for
reward. Martín López desired an appointment as councilman in
Mexico City or some other post in the king's service for either
himself or his son.[19] However, any consideration of the realities
of the moment suggests the unlikelihood of his realizing his hope.
By 1560 the councilmen of Mexico City counted scarcely a single
conquistador among their number, and the pattern of replacement
for those who had died or resigned suggested a heavy emphasis
upon inheritance by sons of former councilmen. Furthermore,
the social position of councilmen was such, by the mid-1560's,
that a son of a former viceroy was happy to be so designated.[20]
Perhaps the man whose early services had been so underestimated
by others had now clearly come to overestimate his worth to
king and colony!

The date of marriage of Martín López Ossorio to Beatriz
de Ribera is not known, but their wedding did serve to ally
two prominent conquistadors, for Beatriz was the daughter of
Gerónimo López and Mencia de Ribera.[21] Gerónimo had been
secretary of the audiencia (and as such had hampered Martín
López in 1533 in his litigation with Maldonado) and later saw
service as councilman of Mexico City. The descendants of Beatriz
and Martín the younger could be equally proud of both conquistador grandfathers.

[18] López, 1528-1574, pp. 151-52, 167, 171, 180, Conway Coll. (Aberdeen).
[19] Ibid., 153.        [20] Actas de cabildo, VII, 216, 298.
[21] Martín López Ossorio, 92-95, Conway Coll. (LC).

Despite the potentialities of young Martín López Ossorio and the wedded bliss Juana might have known with Francisco Pérez del Castillo, the woes that beset the conquistador and all the other members of the López family in 1560 were so numerous and so real that any prospect of relief from them was eagerly awaited.

CHAPTER X

PATTERNS FOR ENDLESS TOMORROWS

ITH promise of more in the years ahead, Viceroy Velasco and Archbishop Montúfar, by 1560, had successfully completed a decade in New Spain. For the conquistador element, however, it was a different matter. Although still numerous and strong, it had passed its peak in the affairs of New Spain.

In Puebla, Alonso Galeote and Pedro de Villanueva held on, but fellow veterans and citizens Martín de Calahorra and Francisco de Oliveros had both died during the past decade. The former's encomienda in Tlaxcala, with its appraised income of 800 pesos annually, had passed to a son. In like fashion a son of Francisco de Oliveros held in the same district the encomienda of his father, property with an appraised income of 660 pesos annually.[1] Such was essentially the story throughout the land: some conquistadors were yet alive; others had perpetuated their interests and outlooks in their heirs. Nowhere was this more clearly the case than in Mexico City.

Sometime after mid-1558 a long-term councilman of the vice-regal capital, Ruy González, was removed by death. The dawn of the next decade witnessed his half-Indian daughter and her Spanish husband, Francisco de Nava, fighting in the courts for the right to retain Ruy's encomiendas for themselves and their six legitimate offspring.[2]

The summer of 1559 brought death to Bernardino Vázquez de Tapia, closing the career of a conquistador who had been active full thirty-five years, the last ten of which found him the senior member of the cabildo of Mexico City. The early 1560 count of encomiendas in New Spain listed the doughty veteran's properties, representing almost 3,000 pesos income yearly, in the hands of his son.[3] Man of many talents, he had so lived as to put the imprint of Spanish culture significantly upon the face of the emergent colonial life of New Spain.

Occasionally a conquistador was still to be found among the councilmen and alcaldes of the viceregal capital, but time had conspired to reduce their importance. From the 1520's, when they had monopolized municipal posts, to midcentury, when they still dominated the scene with an appreciable number of respected, perpetual officeholders, the conquistador element had declined sharply in numbers and influence. After 1560 it was a rarity to find one of the earliest veterans in the cabildo, though here, as with the encomiendas, it was often a matter of the sons of the conquistadors following in the footsteps of their fathers.

Not all the dying conquistadors had distinguished records in the manner of González and Vázquez de Tapia. Alonso de Contreras, a Narváez veteran who died in 1559, was the husband of

---

[1] Paso y Troncoso, *Epistolario de Nueva España*, IX, 11, 12, 23, 31; González de Cossío, *El libro de las tasaciones*, 609-10.

[2] Información de Ruy González (1558), Paso y Troncoso Coll., Leg. 94; Paso y Troncoso, IX, 28, 35.

[3] *Actas de cabildo*, VI, 364; Paso y Troncoso, IX, 20, 36; González de Cossío, 511-12.

a woman of quality. They were the parents of fourteen children. So poor was this conquistador that he was not only without the means to provide his daughters with dowries, but he even lacked sufficient income to support them. Contreras insisted shortly before his death that he needed 3,000 pesos yearly to maintain his household. With his passing, his encomienda in Oaxaca, yielding scarcely one-tenth that amount, went to a son.[4]

Other conquistadors with large families and an attendant concern about dowries were Alonso Pérez de Zamora, an archer who had served aboard a brigantine during the siege of Tenochtitlán, and Martín de la Mezquita, a long-term resident of Antequera, Oaxaca, and like López a native of Andalusia and one of his old friends. The problem of the needy conquistador with numerous daughters crying out for dowries was commonplace—in Mexico City, Antequera, and off on the Pacific slope as well. There in Colima in 1558 Juan Fernández was more than mildly concerned about his dowryless daughters of marriageable age.[5]

Other conquistadors went on living. Pedro de Meneses, holding the encomienda of Coyuca in Michoacán and the encomiendas of Chicoaque and Tequepilpa in Tlaxcala with their annual aggregate yield of about 1,800 pesos income, was one of the last of the original veterans to serve Mexico City in the role of alcalde mayor.[6]

As the conquistadors passed on, they bequeathed their attitudes and properties to wives, sons, and daughters. According to the statement of January, 1560, regarding the encomiendas then held in New Spain, of a total of 375 encomenderos holding 345 property grants (some persons held more than one encomienda and on other occasions several held a single encomienda) fewer than

[4] Información de Alonso de Contreras (1531, 1537, 1559), Paso y Troncoso Coll., Leg. 93; Paso y Troncoso, IX, 15.

[5] Información de los méritos y servicios de Alonso Pérez de Zamora (1540, 1559, 1583), Paso y Troncoso Coll., Leg. 96; Información de Martín de la Mezquita (1540, 1559, 1573), ibid., Leg. 95; Información de Juan Fernández (1558), ibid., Leg. 94.

[6] Actas de cabildo, VI, 437; Paso y Troncoso, IX, 9; González de Cossío, 146-49, 171-73.

25 percent were in the hands of conquistadors.[7] Slightly more than 30 percent of the encomiendas were held in 1560 by the sons of the original grantees.

Some few conquistadors possessed estates which they bequeathed to two or more heirs. Alonso de Ávila, a Grijalva man and an early captain of Cortés whose services had included escorting royal treasure to Spain—treasure which fell into the hands of French pirates—and the subsequent supplying of lime for the construction of numerous early public buildings of Mexico City, bequeathed one encomienda to a son-in-law and another, the better, to his son. Wealthy Leonel de Cervantes also divided his estate, widow and son sharing it. By 1560 the encomienda of Guillén de la Loa, long years dead, had been divided between his widow and their grandson, who had succeeded to his father's interest.[8] Several others also divided their estates.

Many widows of conquistadors directly held encomiendas in 1560. Some such, having taken second husbands, naturally encouraged these men, who commonly were themselves latecomers, to adopt the conquistador outlook on such issues as that of the perpetual encomienda. In similar fashion encomienda-carrying daughters saw their chances at matrimony improved and the outlook of their conquistador fathers perpetuated in the sons-in-law they had not lived to know. When Gonzalo Portillo succeeded to Andrés Núñez' half interest in the encomienda of Tequixquiac by his marriage to Núñez' daughter, still another young man shared the attitudes which his father-in-law long had entertained. The fact that Portillo had as his fellow encomendero at Tequixquiac oldtimer Martín López underscored still more the prospect of the survival of the old outlook.

The tendency of the crown was to reduce, if not eliminate, the encomiendas. One thing constantly before the thinning group of veterans and their heirs was the realization that heirless property

---

[7] This analysis is derived from Paso y Troncoso, IX, 2-43.

[8] Información de los méritos y servicios de Alonso de Ávila (1531), Paso y Troncoso Coll., Leg. 93; Información de los méritos y servicios de Guillén de la Loa (1543), *ibid.*, Leg. 95.

holders could expect their grants to revert to the crown. By 1560 a considerable number of such specific cases had occurred. So it was that he who was an heir developed anew the Spaniard's great concern for legality and treasured among his richest possessions those old documents of the earliest decades which validated the family's original grants.

Many conquistadors were still holders of their own encomiendas. The single, incomplete list of 1560 records among the living a full half-hundred encomienda-holding conquistadors. Martín López, holding one-half of the pueblo of Tequixquiac in encomienda, shared the income which, in 1560, was estimated at 1,600 pesos, paid in money and in maize and other grains.

Martín López definitely was not alone as he, already in his seventies, shuffled into the 1560's. Yet our knowledge of his last years is sketchy.

On March 23, 1561, Bernardino Ossorio of Seville indicated, as he prepared to cross to New Spain, that he was going to the Indies to live with Martín López.[9] Knowing the generous nature of the conquistador, one feels this expectant youth out of Spain was welcomed to the household in Mexico City, even though López' position was not such as to promote the prospects of any young and ambitious kinsman. In truth he was not the first of the family to leave Spain to join López in America, Bernaldino Ossorio, one of his witnesses in 1560, having been a member of his household for many years.[10]

A year later, on April 8, 1562, the father appealed to the throne with the request that a son of his be appointed to one of the canonries then vacant in the churches in Mexico City or Puebla. Accompanying the petition on behalf of a son was a report of his own services in the conquest.[11] The vagueness that finds López failing to mention the son by name derives, at least in part, from the fact he had more than one son seeking a career in the church. All three of his cleric-minded offspring matured and sought

[9] Misc. Docs., 2, Conway Coll. (Cambridge).
[10] López, 1528-1574, pp. 171-72, Conway Coll. (Aberdeen).
[11] Ibid., 188.

church posts during the years of Archbishop Alonso de Montúfar's administration of the archdiocese. That churchman busied himself not only with the propagation of the faith but also with the purification of the clergy, and accordingly, young men lacking in self-discipline could, in the years of his leadership, feel increasingly ill at ease in church service. The fact that López' sons entered upon clerical careers and remained steadfast is perhaps in itself an indirect indication of the morally upright and disciplined homelife to which they had been accustomed.

It was unusual for three sons of one family to enter the clergy. López' financial straits and the very dim prospect of their knowing real improvement might have helped to dictate the choice of careers. Also the essentially Christian nature of the conquistador himself must account in considerable measure for the acceptance by his sons of the reasonableness of such a career. López might also have been responding to Archbishop Montúfar's appeal for more and more clergymen to meet the demands of the church in New Spain.

Archiepiscopal records of the early 1560's, echoing those of the previous decade, repeatedly speak of the shortage of clergy in the land. Even as he reported happily, on July 16, 1561, that the "Lutheran pestilence" had not touched New Spain, the archbishop dolefully related that the ratio of clergymen to population in New Spain was such that not one-tenth of what the church should do was being done, that in broad populous districts no clergymen were available. Surely it was to be expected that the spiritual leader of New Spain would address his king on such a religious problem, but so, on occasion, did Hernando Cortés' son, the second marquis of the Valley. Early in 1564 Martín Cortés addressed his monarch with the request that he send more friars to New Spain, citing particularly the shortage of Franciscans in the land.[12]

In 1562 López petitioned the cabildo of Mexico City for a building lot in the San Pablo district on the channel of water

[12] Paso y Troncoso, IX, 132-33; X, 12-13.

which passed by the church of the same name. The municipal authorities granted the conquistador's request, with the stipulation that he erect a house there within a stated interval.[13] Whether this was to become a new residence for the conquistador and his family or merely constituted an income-producing venture is not clear, but in all likelihood the latter was the case, it being commonplace for men of means in Mexico City to hold rental properties.

As had happened many times earlier, Mexico City in 1562 was very busy with the task of formulating instructions and readying procurators for a trip to Spain in behalf of its citizens. The forty-six announced subjects, as well as a smaller number of related secret instructions, mirrored the outlook of the most insistent conquistador. First, for example, was their resolute request that the crown confer the encomienda rights in perpetuity, an idea which also loomed first among the secret items. The second instruction on the long list urged that the sons of conquistadors be accorded special attention and solicitude by the crown. Complaint was leveled at the high and still-rising prices of linens, silks, wines, and other merchandise. Special consideration for the sons of conquistadors was sought in connection with vacant church posts.

Daughters of conquistadors likewise drew attention. In 1562 it was claimed that more than 2,000 marriageable daughters of conquistadors and early settlers of the city were not married, and because the financial status of their fathers did not permit the necessary dowries, it was likely most of them would follow the footsteps of other frustrated females and enter the convents of the city. Another unhappy product of the socially dictated dowry so many fathers could not afford was the marked rise in clandestine marriages.

Cognizance was taken of the fact that often a man hied himself to Europe for a bride and a place of residence. That ugly practice doubly hurt New Spain, for it doomed even more marriageable maids to solitary lives while removing Spanish family potential so needed in the widening settlement of the land.

[13] *Actas de cabildo*, VII, 89.

The cabildo also deplored the relationship between the great number of unmarried yet marriageable young women in New Spain and the exorbitant expenses related to the dowry, the cost of apparel, and the other heavy financial outlays attendant upon marriage. Distressed by the seriousness of the matter in the life of the colony, the authorities besought enforcement of earlier royal decrees on the subject.[14]

With his encomienda, his sons, and his unmarried daughters, Martín López surely was a party to the wave of sentiment in Mexico City out of which such municipal instructions were born.

Luis de Velasco, who died the next year, assigned a caballería of land to the 75-year-old López within the pueblo of Huehuetoca in 1563. Close by the marker separating Huehuetoca from the pueblo of Zitaltepeque, this property lay between Mexico City and Tequixquiac, not far south of the latter and near the López-held inn site in the pueblo of Cuautitlán. Speedily the status of the land, held to be unencumbered by Corregidor Constantino Bravo de Lagunas, who conducted an investigation for the viceroy, was challenged by natives of the region. López scarcely had had the soil worked and seeded when natives of the pueblo of Huehuetoca took their challenge of the legality of his title to the viceroy. The viceroy ordered Graviel de Chaves, corregidor of the pueblo of Atitalaquia, to conduct an investigation in September of that year and submit his conclusions and recommendations regarding the true status of the disputed caballería of land.

In the spring of the following year, the conquistador appealed Corregidor Chaves' recommendation that the caballería be divided between the Indians and himself, terming it unjust. Pointing out that he had not exceeded his rights, that he had made immediate and meaningful use of the land, that half a caballería was an uneconomic amount of land to work, that he had a large number of children to support, and that the present dispute had already cost him more than one hundred pesos, López sought justice, a term which to him was synonymous in this instance with clear title

14 *Ibid.*, VI, 35-48; VII, 59, 62-66.

to the entire caballería and release from the costs of litigation
he had sustained.[15]

The final outcome of this land dispute is not known, but quite
clear is the revelation that time had neither curtailed López'
interests nor altered his outlook.

In marked contrast to the vigor of the septuagenarian shipwright was the physical debility which had visited itself upon
conquistador councilmen Antonio de Carvajal and Gerónimo
López. The same sun-drenched April that witnessed don Martín's
fight for the entire caballería at Huehuetoca found Carvajal and
Gerónimo López physically unable to attend cabildo sessions.
The former complained of generally poor health; the latter,
having recently been bled, could not marshal the strength needed
to go to the cabildo session. For both, May was like April.[16]
For both, the end that spelled still further reduction of conquistador strength was not far distant.

Even closer to his earthly end was Viceroy Velasco, death
coming for him on July 31, 1564. In the wake of his demise all
New Spain knew restless moments.

Despite the high cost of living and worries about careers for
his sons and dowries for his daughters, Martín López surely must
have counted the Velasco years better than those under the first
viceroy. And he might have viewed the future with apprehension.
At a time in life when he knew he had but few more earthly
days, it must have been agonizing to him to realize that all his
unfinished business would now fall into the hands of another
viceroy fresh from Spain, a person whose cultivation would
require perhaps more time than he or any other conquistador
might have at his disposal.

Weeks slipped into months, the year passed, and with mid-1565

[15] Mercedes, VI, fol. 21; VII, fol. 105v; Pedimiento de Martín López, April
23 (?), 1564, privately owned by Manuel Romero de Terreros, Mexico City. The
writer gratefully acknowledges the cooperation of don Manuel Romero de Terreros,
who generously supplied him with a copy of this document concerning the very
existence of which he otherwise would have remained ignorant.

[16] Actas de cabildo, VII, 191, 195, 207.

A López Petition of April 23 (?), 1564

*Reproduction of the opening and close of a manuscript held by*
*don Manuel Romero de Terreros of Mexico City*

the conquistador had another opportunity to say a good word for services rendered in days of long ago. In July, Francisco de Escobar appeared before the audiencia in Mexico City with a petition and an interrogatory in behalf of the services rendered Spain by the Tlaxcalans during the first half of the sixteenth century. In item sixteen of this concise twenty-four-question interrogatory the Tlaxcalan contributions toward the building and transportation of the prefabricated brigantine fleet were set forth.

Prominent among the witnesses called on behalf of the Indians was shipwright Martín López. Like him, the Tlaxcalans had been promised great things by Cortés. Like López, the treatment accorded the Indian allies had not matched the reward promised. Like the shipwright, the Tlaxcalans, with this action of 1565, went on fighting for the things earned by them and promised to them. The interrogatory served to transport witness López back across forty-five years of the half century he had spent in the New World. A quickened memory gave warm support to the contentions of the natives.[17]

Two years later, López had kind words for a viceroy about to lose his post. Following the death of Viceroy Velasco in mid-1564 and the interim exercise of authority by the audiencia, don Gaston de Peralta, marquis of Falces, had been designated third viceroy of New Spain late in 1566. In that two-year interval in the mid-1560's occurred a rebellion in which Martín Cortés, second marquis of the Valley of Oaxaca, became a pivotal personality. A wave of creole discontent threatened Spanish authority in New Spain. Cloaked in secrecy which has defied scholars ever since, the revolt has continued to be a subject of speculation to the present.

The rebellious elements had been ferreted out and dealt with by the audiencia before the arrival of the third viceroy. However, a trumped-up case of collusion between the outgoing rebels and the incoming viceroy caused the suspension of the newly named official.

[17] "Información recibida en México y Puebla el año de 1565," *Biblioteca Histórica de la Iberia*, XX (1875), 13-26, 113-22.

With an honest man trapped by the machinations of masters of political intrigue, a number of the doughty old conquistadors rose as a man in December, 1567, in defense of the marquis of Falces. It was then that eleven fairminded veterans of the conquest informed Philip II that the audiencia had crushed the rebellion and that the marquis of Falces was governing a tranquil land in pursuit of the royal interests. They said the removal of the viceroy was being prompted by false information against him. Among the signers, the name of Martín López stood second. Their bold letter, however, did not stay the bureaucratic will, for the third viceroy soon left for Spain under a cloud of royal suspicion early in 1568.[18] López, the letter signer of 1567, was about eighty years of age.

A month later, on January 29, 1568, the discredited marquis of Falces granted López' eldest son two caballerías of land within the pueblo of Tequixquiac.[19]

Entering New Spain in 1568 and remaining there for twelve years, Viceroy Martín Enríquez outlasted most of the remaining conquistadors. Even as he first put foot ashore on New Spain, the new viceroy had figured in an action which sharpened the focus of international attention directed at the Spanish New World. John Hawkins and his cousin Francis Drake had preceded the viceroy to Vera Cruz and, having dropped the anchors of their nine vessels, were ready to repair unseaworthy ships and engage in illicit commerce when the viceroy's thirteen-vessel fleet hove into sight. A truce enabled the Spanish ships to land, but once ashore and in command of the situation, Viceroy Enríquez immediately attacked the English shipping, seizing all but two of the vessels. Fanning the flames of English hatred for all things Spanish, this episode influenced the new viceroy's outlook and program. Year after year, major attention was directed to securing

[18] Paso y Troncoso, X, 215-17; Hubert Howe Bancroft, *History of Mexico* (6 vols., San Francisco, 1883-1888), II, 602-32; Alonso de Montúfar, *Descripción del Arzobispado de México hecha en 1570 y otros documentos*, ed. by Luis García Pimentel (Mexico City, 1897), 380.

[19] Mercedes, IX, fol. 279.

the frontiers of his viceroyalty: garrisons were assigned and fortresses built at Vera Cruz, Acapulco, and elsewhere on the Gulf and Pacific coasts, and an expedition was sent against the vigorous Chichimecas on the northern frontier.[20]

Meanwhile, Archbishop Alonso de Montúfar, in the spring of 1566, had inaugurated a long-term survey of the Archbishopric of Mexico. Primarily intended as a check on the clergy, their practices, and their charges, the survey included the best extant statistical summary of López' Tequixquiac region.

In late October, 1569, the parish priest of Tequixquiac had instructions to assemble certain information. He reported that the pueblo of Tequixquiac, in which Martín López' encomienda was located, contained 172 houses and the following population: 301 married citizens, 17 widowers, 35 widows, 9 unmarried males older than fourteen years; and 7 unmarried females older than twelve years, as well as 319 children. The town had a church dedicated to Santiago, in which the clergyman conducted worship when not in the nearby pueblos of Apasco and Tlapanaloya, which were also assigned to him. No tension or trouble between the priest and either the corregidor of Citlaltepeque or encomenderos Martín López and Gonzalo Portillo was reported. Expecting the natives of Tequixquiac to appear on Sundays and feast days for instruction in catechism, the priest apparently had the fullest cooperation of encomendero Martín López, for no word of complaint was uttered against the conquistador. With only two or three Spaniards in the entire area, the creole priest who had been born in Mexico City was linguistically equipped for his charge with a command of the Otomí and Nahuatl tongues.[21]

Archbishop Montúfar's survey, which touched so marginally upon the interests of the conquistador encomendero, had a direct bearing upon the career of López' priestly son Agustín. In late 1569 Agustín López, serving the pueblo of Tlalchichilpa and its environs as priest, was called upon to supply the same kind of

[20] Paso y Troncoso, X, 260-61, 278-89.
[21] Montúfar, 43, 66-72, 306-308, 312, 317, 322-23.

information that had been offered for the region in which Martín López' encomienda was located. At an annual salary of 150 pesos, which was paid by an encomendero and supplemented modestly by several ranchers, Padre Agustín López superintended the religious life of the pueblo of Tlalchichilpa and a score of nearby lesser communities. His charge lay some eleven leagues west of Mexico City and within two leagues of Toluca. With a bare handful of Spaniards in the area, he was preeminently concerned with the scattered and almost barbarous Indians of the region. Although he had a command of Nahuatl, he was hampered in his efforts to lead his parishioners by his ignorance of the Mazahua language.

The magnitude of the task before the 29-year-old priest, as well as the lofty aims he entertained, can be sensed from the measure of derogatory comment he offered in his report. The alcalde mayor, with headquarters in Toluca, was charged with neglecting his duties, even failing to visit some of the pueblos under his supervision. Consequently, justice was poorly administered among the people the priest served. Not one to thrust blame solely upon others, Agustín added that his inability to use the Mazahua tongue reduced his capacity to administer church affairs. Having written his report, Agustín López appeared in Mexico City on December 2, 1569, before Dr. Esteban de Portillo with his credentials. From them it is evident he had been ordained "de corona" on December 18, 1556, at age sixteen. On June 8, 1560, he had been ordained "de evangelio." Seven years later the bishop of Tlaxcala ordained him "de misa" on September 20, 1567. A license to sing masses, signed by the archbishop, was accorded him on December 4, 1567.[22] Such was the pattern of one conquistador's son's progress in the church.

By 1570 Agustín López had drawn commendation from the archbishop himself. On April 11 of that year the foremost churchman of the land described Agustín as "a very worthy priest, son of one of the first conquistadors of this country, and himself

[22] *Ibid.*, 153-61, 331.

virtuous, modest, and of exemplary life," one who had performed and was still engaged in clerical labors among the natives of New Spain. Because of his background, his good qualities, his clerical record, and his knowledge of the native language, the archbishop recommended Agustín to the consideration of the crown as worthy of appointment to any canonry in the cathedrals of the Indies. Well might Agustín López use any such influence in behalf of his clerical career, for his had not been noteworthy advancement over a thirteen-year period. In contrast with his own progress was that of his acquaintance Pedro de la Mota, son of conquistador Gerónimo Ruiz de la Mota. Pedro de la Mota was advanced from ordination "de corona" as of November 27, 1568, to the right to celebrate masses granted in a license dated June 4, 1569. In less than one year the professional achievement of Pedro de la Mota matched the thirteen-year effort of Agustín López[23]

To elderly Martín López, moving into his middle eighties, it must have been particularly pleasing to know that a powerful personage stood as his ally in his continuous search for opportunities for his children.

Even as he hoped for his own son's advancement in the church, López was ever ready to help another. In the course of Dr. Esteban de Portillo's efforts to verify the purity of his lineage, as he sought advancement within the church in 1571-1572, the former shipwright was called as a witness. In Mexico City on December 10, 1571, 84-year-old Martín López, "who built the brigantines with which the city was won," testified in behalf of Portillo, son of a fellow conquistador, as he answered his eleven-item interrogatory. The churchman's father, Francisco Portillo, had entered New Spain with Cortés and, with his wife María Ximenez, had been among the earliest settlers of Puebla. A creole priest renowned for his prudence, rectitude, powers of concentration, and broad experience, this superiorly educated son of a conquistador had drawn such commendation from the archbishop as to suggest his had been possibly the most successful career of

[23] *Ibid.*, 380; López, 1528-1574, p. 189, Conway Coll. (Aberdeen).

any of the sons of conquistadors dedicated to the spiritual needs of New Spain. With Dr. Portillo a particularly prominent churchman of Mexico City in the 1570's, any good word in his behalf by Martín López did no harm to the López trio in the service of the church.[24]

About 1572 eldest son Martín López Ossorio took action which suggested the end was near for his father. Through attorney Alonso de Herrera, young Martín petitioned the throne for a warrant which would assist him in continuing to receive favor and appointments from viceroys after the death of his father. With the double likelihood that his conquistador parent might die at any time and he as first-born and heir would have nothing more than the paltry grant held by his father, this married creole son was seriously concerned about his own future, lest he "fall heir to the dreary condition of poverty and privation in which his father has lived and is still living." Buttressing his request, the son sent a certified copy of his father's twelve-year-old petition of 1560 to Spain.[25]

Despite such fears regarding his well-being, the conquistador went on living. In 1573 he testified in support of the contentions of Luis and Juan Suárez de Peralta in a suit in Mexico City. Late that year, on October 6, the aged conquistador served as witness in behalf of the plea directed to the crown by a son of fellow conquistador Martín de la Mezquita.[26] This is the last definitely dated act in the life of aged and weary Martín López. Like so many other acts that had punctuated his career in New Spain, this last one was yet another warm and friendly expression of his continuing identification with the interests of the conquistador class.

Death came to don Martín sometime between late 1573 and the petition of January 17, 1577, by his son Martín López Ossorio.[27]

[24] Mexico, Doc. XXXI, fols. 15-16, Harkness Coll. (LC); Paso y Troncoso, XI, 73-74, 126-27, 143-44, 238-39, 242-43, 255; XII, 21, 52.

[25] López, 1528-1574, pp. 147-87, Conway Coll. (Aberdeen).

[26] Conway, *La Noche Triste*, 86; Información de Martín de la Mezquita (1540, 1559, 1573), Paso y Troncoso Coll., Leg. 95.

[27] Porras Muñoz, "Martín López," in *Estudios Cortesianos*, 319n56.

As with his birth, López' death is shrouded in a three-year period of uncertainty. By the middle 1570's the conquistador had lived well into the terms of the fourth viceroy and the third archbishop of New Spain. A man who had helped to inaugurate the intrusion of Spain into New Spain had lived long enough to witness the consolidation of well-nigh every aspect of the life of that colony.

In a period replete with change, at least one thing went unchanged. Finally, on May 7, 1574, when royal action was taken on López' petition of 1560 seeking the post of councilman, the decision, "This request cannot be granted," found the conquistador once again unrewarded.[28] By the time this delayed decision reached New Spain, there is strong likelihood the shipwright-hidalgo of Seville and Mexico City had gone to his final reward.

[28] López, 1528-1574, p. 187, Conway Coll. (Aberdeen).

## CHAPTER XI

## A MAN IN A MEMORABLE MOMENT

OUT OF the long career of Martín López emerges a view of the role of the conquistador citizen in New Spain. The average conquistador made a twofold contribution to history. In his short, dramatic, well-known first phase, that which too commonly is considered his total role, he was a warrior-destroyer, the wrecker of native cultures. In his second, longer, and more complex phase of activity, he was a citizen-creator, the founder of a new way of life in the Americas.

Just as the late fifteenth-century Spain of which he was heir had been a complex of social, economic, political, and religious forces, as well as military actions, so too the New World conquistador was a mixture of moods and motives. Simultaneously a product of his Spanish past and a response to New World challenges, he was a modified European, a Spaniard in transition who moved through the years of late Middle Ages and early Renaissance under the special impact of frontier conditions in the New World.

The personal yearnings within Martín López, as with every other individual conquistador, dictated the initial move that led him across the Atlantic to the Indies. Ambitious to achieve name and position that circumstances within his family and Spain itself denied him at home, his search for personal advancement caused him to join the conquistador class in America. With nobles and other fine figures of Spanish society seldom in the ranks of the conquistadors, the men who expanded the Spanish empire were basically a hungering lot of ambition-driven young Spaniards of depressed social and economic position.

The ambition of the conquistador was complemented by a nature simultaneously courageous and aggressive, qualities which were both positive and negative. The admirable refusal to accept the limitations of life in Spain and the courage that braved wide waters and unknown lands were combined with despicable aggressiveness which robbed, exploited, enslaved, and killed the natives of the New World. All came from the greed-tinged nature of the aggressive, courageous conquistador.

Wealth was the catalyst that could bring prestige and power to the individual conquistador, and his rapacious pursuit of it made greed an elementary aspect of his nature. Loot-laden Spaniards offered their lives on the altar of greed as they died on the causeways of Tenochtitlán during the withdrawal of the Sad Night; and plundering Spaniards so individually had pocketed the wealth of the Aztecs that the meager public distribution of booty was anticlimactic. Whenever building lots, gardening plots, ranching sites, and encomiendas were allotted, Martín López, like every other surviving conquistador, stood with hand outstretched, such being a natural posture for men who had won the land in a free-lance, private adventure. Moreover, the inordinate pursuit of wealth that spelled greed produced many monuments to the generous, self-sacrificing nature of the conquistador class: chapels, schools, orphanages, and organizations dedicated to works smacking of genuine social consciousness.

The conquistadors who were rapacious in years of warfare quite commonly lived out decades of harmonious relations with the Indians of New Spain. At one moment they raped Indian women and killed Indian men; on other occasions they recognized their illegitimate children, married their Indian favorites, fostered the conversion of their encomienda-held Indians, and appealed to the crown for recognition and reward of Indian services during the conquest.

Paradoxical, too, was the loyalty of the conquistadors. Initially bound to Governor Velázquez of Cuba, Cortés and his followers cast aside that loyalty. Initially loyal to Cortés, Cristóbal de Olid and many others cast that loyalty aside. Yet the rebellious conquistadors remained ever loyal to their king and to themselves, and in so doing, they were both generous and greedy all over again.

The conquistador who seemed to depend only upon his own strong right arm placed great dependence upon his God. Part of the courage that led him into battles outnumbered 20, 50, even 100 to one was a matter of the spirit. Happily, the purposes of church and man combined in the campaigns which found the material appetites of the conquistador for loot and land and laborers joined by ecclesiastical insistence that the Indians be converted to the ranks of Catholicism. Economically, the indolent Spaniard, dedicated to shunning manual labor, had to promote the survival of the native population; spiritually, that survival of the Indian element was a challenge to the orthodox religion he had brought from Spain.

Culturally, the robust conquistador transplanted the social hierarchy, the economic order, the political system, the religious faith of Spain as rapidly as he could in the New World. Essentially, the simple-appearing conquistador citizen was endlessly complex, with the career of Martín López not unrepresentative of the paradoxical pattern of the group in which he proudly claimed membership.

Crossbowman and swordsman, infantryman and cavalryman, worker and warrior, López had contributed to the conquest in ways that stamped him civilian as well as fighter, a man of brain as well as brawn.

For a half century of civilian life, López identified himself closely with Mexico City. As a citizen with varied interests rooted in the community and with a growing family to promote widening concern about many aspects of urban life, López was one fighter turned civilian who helped to put the Hispanic stamp upon the life of the most important center of population of New Spain as he acquired property under terms of Spanish law, as he bought and sold goods at prices related to Spanish monetary units, as he appeared for his share of recurring allotments of land to the citizenry, as he registered a sheep brand with municipal authorities, as he fought for his rights in Spanish-imported courts, as he had his children baptized—as, in fact, he lived every little detail of a life strangely new to the land in which he resided. López was endlessly loyal to the agencies of government, all the way from cabildo to crown and back again through council to corregidor. As a resident of Mexico City, Martín López was a common citizen whose daily life helped add up to the uncommon thing that was the transference of European culture to continental America.

Economic position, one of the most persistent pursuits of the conquistador, is peculiarly difficult to assess in the career of Martín López. Emerging as he did from the conquest with some wealth, one wonders how much of it related to that military experience and how much was a carryover of prior holdings. In addition to acquiring building lots, gardening plots, caballerías, ranching establishments, and an encomienda, he was a party to numerous commercial transactions, definitely pursued sheep raising, and engaged at least indirectly in mining enterprises. In addition to the fact that his contribution to the conquest deserved recognition, López had financial ends in view when he entered suits against Cortés. Willing to enter Cortés' service without specific promise of reward, as did all the men, he had a keen awareness of his worth when success attended the enterprise. At one moment wealthy enough to spend more than 10,000 pesos on the New Galicia campaign, he shortly thereafter was so poor for decades as to be the object of special concern by his friends and acquaintances. With ample means he lived in dignity, generous to friend and stranger; without adequate means he was unable to meet the needs of his own children. Able to afford a dowry for but one of his five daughters, only the eldest girl was well married. Poverty kept Juana's sisters in seclusion. Direct relationship might even exist between Martín López' reduced economic status and the number of sons serving the church.

In his appeals for posts, his statements of penury, his search for funds to provide dowries, his admission that sons lived away from home because he lacked means to maintain and educate them properly, one senses extreme want. Yet the continued pursuit by López of a gentlemanly way of life—keynoted by leisure rather than continuous identification with economic endeavors—leads one to suspect some measure of the hardship was more imaginary than real, a relative thing in reference to the social setting of Mexico City, a comparative thing for one who had known opulence. At a time when petitions and litigation were far from expense-free, this man who never won a court battle strangely continued with the means to support another courtroom effort, another petition. In the final analysis, López' economic plight, as well as his complaints on that score, can best be appreciated only in relation to the society in which he moved. This man, who received a pittance from his encomienda, no income of record from his other interests, and no apparent remuneration for services between the distribution of the booty in the early 1520's and the payment of his salary as corregidor in 1556, maintained himself and his family in Mexico City in such fashion as to indicate they did not move on the lowest social levels.

Of hidalgo background himself, Martín López twice married Spanish ladies of like status, founding with his second wife one of the earliest large creole families of Mexico City. In a day in which men were unashamed of their extramarital relations and even recognized their illegitimate mestizo offspring, there is no mention of any such liaisons by López, no second family on the margin of respectability hastening the amalgamation of the population of New Spain. López counted as close friends many of the men serving in the highest municipal posts, men such as Gerónimo Ruiz de la Mota, into whose family López' grandson married, Gerónimo López, whose daughter married Martín's eldest son, and Antonio de Carvajal and Bernardino Vázquez de Tapia, fellow conquistadors with considerable antipathy of their own for Cortés. On still higher levels of government, López included among his friends such persons as Gonzalo Cerezo, alguacil mayor of the audiencia, Factor Hernando de Salazar, of great influence in the 1540's, and Tristán de Luna y Arellano, confidant and aide of successive viceroys.

No small matter in the life of Martín López was the element of pride. He was proud of his heritage and that of his wives; and he was proud of his conquistador role and of his children. He proudly bequeathed certain glorious memories to later generations as he sought and obtained one coat of arms after another. The marriage of his creole son Martín to a creole girl named Beatriz de Ribera was no accident, nor was it accidental that his creole daughter Juana married a creole boy named Francisco Pérez del Castillo. Lest the seeming jealousy with which he guarded the purity of Spanish blood in the family be construed as supercilious haughtiness or blind racial hatred, recall that López was one encomendero whose handling of his Indians drew no condemnation from passing investigators. He likewise was one who so understood and admired the natives that he gladly and warmly extolled their individual and collective conquest services. If in López' nature there be clear-cut support for the idea of social stratification, it plainly was not the unhealthy, prejudice-ridden attitude of the latecomer whose ignorance and arrogance often paved paths of lingering ill will between the races.

As in his relations with less fortunate Spaniards, López felt a
sense of responsibility in his relations with the Indians that was
akin to social conscience—despite, possibly even because of, his
desire to pass his encomienda on to his son and to his son's son.
This humane side of López is particularly evident in his handling
of the encomienda of Tequixquiac. Possessed of a very small
number of Indians, he could have oppressed them in an effort to
better his financial position. Instead, he seemed to appreciate the
physical limitations imposed by the thinness of the soil, the pattern
of rainfall, and the frequency of killing frosts, satisfying himself,
in consequence, with the small income their labors provided him.
Such behavior by López might have been a partial reflection of
his religious nature.

In a quiet, persistent way Martín López was a Catholic influence
in the life of New Spain. Extreme orthodoxy characterized the
spiritual side of this otherwise not-so-orthodox individual. Descended from an old Christian family himself, López married into
like-minded families. The baptism of his own children and his
willingness to serve as godfather for the children of friends
indicate his religious conformity. At a moment when his action
might be construed as purely partisan, narrowly selfish, and
bitterly anti-Cortés, López' steps to protect certain Indian villages
in Tehuantepec in 1529 could have sprung, in part, from his
consciousness of the dignity and worth of the natives. The absence
of criticism of López' handling of Indian affairs in Tehuantepec
in 1529 and in Tlasco those years he served as corregidor suggest
he pursued policies sufficiently humane as to represent applied
Christianity. An enemy of López was constrained to remark in
Tehuantepec that Alcalde Mayor Martín López acted more like
a monk than a judge.

This man, who lived in the shadow of the great church on the
principal plaza of Mexico City, who gave three sons to New World
clergy, and who supported the professional interests of a churchman like Dr. Portillo, must have been religious. Quietly so, he
was not a party to the hysteria which condemned the Jewish

conquistador and brigantine builder Hernando Alonso in 1528. Nor did evidence of bigotry appear in him when the Inquisition formally came to Mexico City in 1571.

Unobtrusively, within an emergent community which was the fountainhead of the life of an entire viceroyalty, López lived as one loyal to government, to church, to friends, to family, to self. Yet even as he was logical and predictable, this transplanted Spaniard was also a combination of paradoxes.

So completely the Spaniard that he did not help hasten the racial amalgamation of the Old and New World cultures, he insisted, through the completeness of his continued identification with his heritage, upon a thorough introduction of Spanish culture into New Spain. What he had been in Spain, what he had represented during the conquest, he continued to represent across fifty years of peaceful residence in Mexico City. Out of apparent contradictions in the simplicity and complexity of his nature comes the unifying truth that he was significant because he was so clearly a carrier of civilization in the transference of Spanish culture to New Spain. At first some superficial physical resemblances had led Cortés and his followers to give the name New Spain to the land they conquered. Finally, however, that name stuck to the area, and rightly so, only because the cultural transference which ensued made the region deserving of the name. It took conquistadors along with nonconquistadors many years to guarantee the cultural conquest of the area they initially had won militarily.

With most of the conquistadors young men—hence not far removed from the peaceful paths of childhood and youth—and with many of the men not only preconquest artisans but likewise artisans during the conquest, one concludes that most conquistadors, as they shifted to civilian life, actually were going home—leaving, as it were, their unnatural careers. Finally, then, the telling of the full story of the conquistador as both fighter and settled citizen is but a completion of the circuit that saw him a civilian a second time as he strove to make another Spain of the land in which he lived. Returning to civilian status, the conquistador insisted upon bringing the best of the Old World into his new life; in peace as in war he was a conscious proponent of Spanish culture. In both areas of his life, soldier-wrecker and civilian-creator, he was what he was because of his essentially Spanish nature.

With some members living on for half a decade and others for more than a half century, the conquistador class constituted the first powerful pressure group, the earliest lobby, in American history. Individuals journeyed to Spain, wrote letters, produced statements of their services, petitioned for honors and offices. Spokesmen for groups of men, cities, and entire colonies used an endless array of techniques to further New World interests born of conquistador desires. Out of such the conquistador class emerged socially respected, politically powerful, economically strong, and culturally significant. From their early dominant position they did much to establish basic patterns of legal, economic, and social institutions destined to survive the colonial era.

The agricultural activity that saw many European crops introduced into New Spain, the ranching interests that brought many types of European livestock into the land, commercial activity that occupied so many people, the ceaseless litigation that seemed to involve all, the founding of families, the establishment of religious and educational and charitable institutions—all these, and more, found the conquistador citizen a party to the conscious Hispanization of the life of New Spain.

True to his Old World heritage and his New World nature, Martín López had been such a man.

# CRITICAL ESSAY ON AUTHORITIES

TO DATE, the considerable mass of historical literature related to sixteenth-century Mexico falls, with ever-mounting frequency, into the categories of biographical and institutional studies, sharply focused on one man or the end product of so many men that the essentially human aspect of the institution is lost from view.[1] And even as the focus on captains of conquest and viceroys and audiencias and churchmen has demonstrated the transference of Spanish culture from the Old to the New World, it has been commonplace to minimize, if not totally deny, the oneness of the conquistador who badly bruised the native culture and the settler who injected sizable segments of his Spanish heritage into the land. With none of the numerous biographers of Cortés giving balanced treatment to his full career—it would be better history but poorer drama—it is not strange that lesser men of his company who also spanned the two-phase experience of conquistador and settled citizen have been neglected by historians.

In the absence, then, of broad, yet personalized, writing on the theme of the transference of Spanish culture to the New World, one initially approaches sixteenth-century Mexico through survey accounts such as Manuel Orozco y Berra, *Historia de la dominación española en México* (4 vols., Mexico City, 1938); Niceto de Zamacois, *Historia de Méjico, desde sus tiempos más remotos hasta nuestros dias* (22 vols., Mexico City, 1876-1902); Hubert Howe Bancroft, *History of Mexico* (6 vols., San Francisco, 1883-1888); Vicente Riva Palacio and others, *México a través de los siglos* (5 vols., Mexico City, 1887-1889); and C. H. Haring, *The Spanish Empire in America* (New York, 1947).

---

[1] This brief and selective essay does not include all sources cited in the footnotes, and it manifestly does not embrace all sources consulted.

## Manuscripts

In Rip Van Winkle-like fashion the story of the average conquistador settler whose extended Mexican career can be traced
has been slumbering silently for centuries in the piled-high manuscript records of Spanish and Mexican archives. By varying means
of reproduction some of that wealth has been put into public
repositories and private libraries in many other lands.

In Mexico City the Archivo General de la Nación contains
relevant documents under such section headings as Hospital
de Jesús, Mercedes, Tierras, and Historia. Around the corner, in
another part of the National Palace, the Museo Nacional houses
the rich collection of transcripts executed by Francisco del Paso
y Troncoso from the archival holdings of Spain. Here are *in-
formaciones de méritos y servicios* of conquistadors, papers which
combine records of services with petitions for reward, and thus
reflect both the deeds and the desires of lusty overseas Spaniards.
Here the braggart's boast is tempered by the accompanying testimony of six, ten, or more eyewitnesses. Military prowess, social ties,
economic urges, moral compulsions—indeed, the well-nigh complete man emerges from such records. Across from the National
Palace, the Cathedral of Mexico offers, in the form of baptismal
registers, a vital index to church relation and social station.

In the Archivo de Notarías de México, D. F., the economic
side of man is additionally evident. Contracts, stocks of goods,
terms of partnerships, designation of agents, powers of attorney,
wills, apprenticeships, rentals—the assets and liabilities of the
economic man, dead and alive—spread themselves for investigation
and interpretation. Facilitating the use of such is A. Millares
Carlo and J. I. Mantecón, *Indice y extractos de los protocolos
del Archivo de Notarías de México, D. F.* (2 vols., Mexico City,
1945-1946).

Occasionally, too, as in the case of don Manuel Romero
de Terreros, the Mexican intellectual with a bent that relates
his interests to the sixteenth century holds in his personal archives
significant documents.

In Spain, of course, the documentary fountainhead is the Archivo General de Indias in Seville. From thence came many of the forementioned transcripts of Paso y Troncoso. There in the classifications of Audiencia de México 98, Escribanía de Cámara 178B, Patronato 54-3-1, 57-1-1, and 63-1-15 are documents richly related to the career of Martín López. In Seville, also, are materials now most accessible through the Conway Collection.

Prominent within the late G. R. G. Conway's library on colonial Mexico were scores of volumes of photostats, typescripts, and translations of significant documents. Amassed through more than a quarter century of effort that began in the 1920's, they were once entirely, in varying numbers of copies of each item, in the hands of their owner in Mexico. His policy of sharing that wealth with major institutions, pursued by his heirs as well, has led to large segments of the Conway Collection being deposited with the Library of Congress, Cambridge University, and the University of Aberdeen.

The following material in the Conway Collection concerns the career of Martín López:

(1) Martín López, Conquistador—Documents, 1528-1574. Parts one and two consist of interrogatories and testimony dating from 1528 and 1534 respectively. The unified and certified text of these two parts, dating from 1547, consisted of 48 folios and reposed in the Archivo General de Indias under the classification AGI, Patronato 1-2-4/24 (now 57-1-1). The third and last part of this item, a 1560 statement by López supported by the testimony of seven witnesses, approximated 16 folios in the same archive, classified AGI, Patronato 1-3-10/1 (now 63-1-15). Composing two volumes in the Conway Collection, a volume of transcript and a volume of translation, this is available at Aberdeen in translation only.

(2) Martín López, Conquistador—Documents, 1529-1550. Consisting of two parts, this item includes the Santa Cruz perjury case of 1529 and translated extracts of the Nobiliario of Martín López Ossorio, with the latter discussed below in item "5." This volume is in the Manuscripts Division of the Library of Congress.

(3) Documents Relating to Various Suits. This consists of the records of two related legal actions of the late 1520's: Diego Hernández' suit versus Cortés and the latter's action against certain former judges of the audiencia, with López' interests related to both cases. Transcribed from 67 folios in Seville, the documents are at Cambridge in both transcript and translation, with the translation also at Aberdeen.

(4) Francisco Maldonado contra Martín López, 1533-1539. Covering records of litigation that reach back to 1529, this material originally consisted of 268 folios which, in turn, constitute four volumes of the Conway Collection. Richly illustrating facets of López' postwar career, transcripts of this document are at both Cambridge and Aberdeen.

(5) Nobiliario of Martín López Ossorio. Consisting of 205 folios dating from 1624 and representing a cumulative effort by grandchildren of López, this contains much significant, as well as tangential, data regarding Martín López. The most relevant portion, the first 45 folios, constitutes the second part of Conway Collection item "2" above. The three-volume photostatic copy of the original manuscript is at Aberdeen; the Library of Congress has transcripts of the most pertinent López materials.

(6) Miscellaneous Documents Relating to Martín López and Other Papers. This group of seven items includes: (a) a translation of folios 1-45 of the Nobiliario of Martín López Ossorio, a better translation of which is found in "2" above; (b) a transcript of extracts of "4" above; (c) a translation of same; (d) a partial translation of López-related material published by Francisco Fernández del Castillo in the *Boletín de la Sociedad Mexicana de Geografía y Estadística*, XLIII (1931), 17-40; (e) a photostatic copy of Martín López' testimony of 1565 in behalf of Tlaxcalan services during the conquest as published in *Biblioteca Histórica de la Iberia*, XX (1875), 13-29, 113-22; (f) a translation of *Epistolario de Nueva España, 1505-1818*, I, 136-52; and (g) a transcript of 92 pages of documents from AGI, Patronato 79. This volume is at Cambridge; a similar volume, duplicating all except item (g) is at Aberdeen.

In the aggregate the materials of the Conway Collection constitute the core of this biographical study. Although the present volume is one of the earliest efforts to utilize the Conway Collection, recent bibliographical interest suggests it will be used increasingly in the future.[2]

## Published Primary Sources

For the movement of many of the conquistadors to the Indies, Cristóbal Bermúdez Plata, *Catálogo de pasajeros a Indias durante los siglos XVI, XVII y XVIII* (3 vols., Seville, 1940) is a standard reference work. For the events of the conquest, recourse must be made to the pair of indispensable eyewitness accounts: Hernán Cortés, *Cartas de relación de la conquista de Méjico* (2 vols., Madrid, 1942) and Bernal Díaz del Castillo (Joaquín Ramírez Cabañas, ed.), *Historia verdadera de la conquista de la Nueva España* (3 vols., Mexico City, 1944). The captain general's account is admirably complemented by the version of the common foot soldier. A pinpoint appraisal of a significant and much-debated aspect of the conquest is found in G. R. G. Conway (ed.), *La Noche Triste: Documentos: Segura de la Frontera en Nueva España, año de MDXX* (Mexico City, 1943). For conquest and postconquest years alike, despite sloppy editorial work, the multivolume work of J. F. Pacheco, F. Cárdenas, and others (eds.), *Colección de documentos inéditos relativos al descubrimiento, conquista y organización de las antiguas posesiones de América y Oceanía* (42 vols., Madrid, 1864-1884) must be consulted.

Beginning early in 1524, one of the richest sources of political, economic, social, religious, and cultural data on life in Mexico is available in Mexico [City] Cabildo (Ignacio de Bejarano and others, eds.), *Actas de cabildo de la ciudad de México* (26 vols.,

---

[2] In combination the information in the following bibliographical articles represents the fullest listing of the materials of the Conway Collection: Schafer Williams, "The G. R. G. Conway Collection in the Library of Congress: A Checklist," *Hispanic American Historical Review*, XXXV (1955), 386-97; A. P. Thornton, "The G. R. G. Conway Ms. Collection in the Library of the University of Aberdeen," *ibid.*, XXXVI (1956), 345-47; and J. Street, "The G. R. G. Conway Collection in Cambridge University Library: A Checklist," *ibid.*, XXXVII (1957), 60-81.

Mexico City, 1889-1904). Crowded with miscellaneous information, much of it economic in nature, is Francisco del Paso y Troncoso (comp.), *Epistolario de Nueva España, 1505-1818* (16 vols., Mexico City, 1939-1942). A penetrating, though limited, view of religious life is found in Alonso de Montúfar (Luis García Pimentel, ed.), *Descripción del Arzobispado de México hecha en 1570 y otros documentos* (Mexico City, 1897). For biographical data on many conquistadors, consult La Sociedad de Bibliófilos Españoles, *Nobiliario de conquistadores de Indias* (Madrid, 1892); Francisco A. de Icaza, *Diccionario autobiográfico de conquistadores y pobladores de Nueva España* (2 vols., Madrid, 1923); and Ignacio de Villar Villamil (ed.), *Cedulario heráldico de conquistadores de Nueva España* (Mexico City, 1933).

## Monographs and Articles

Aside from the manuscript and published primary sources, the literature that relates to Martín López is exceedingly limited. In the sixteenth century, during the former shipwright's lifetime, one of the earliest professors at the University of Mexico used data gathered from survivors to expand the historical record of the conquest: Francisco Cervantes de Salazar, *Crónica de la Nueva España* (Madrid, 1914). On the occasion of the four hundredth anniversary of the death of Cortés, one Spaniard's contribution, consisting of documents and interpretation, enlarged the view of López: Guillermo Porras Muñoz, "Martín López, carpintero de ribera," in Instituto Gonzalo Fernández de Oviedo, *Estudios Cortesianos—recopilados con motivo del IV centenario de la muerte de Hernán Cortés (1547-1947)* (Madrid, 1948). More recently, the essay by C. Harvey Gardiner, "Tempest in Tehuantepec, 1529: Local Events in Imperial Perspective," *Hispanic American Historical Review*, XXXV (1955), has treated one climactic episode in the conquistador settler's career. Most recently, the volume by C. Harvey Gardiner, *Naval Power in the Conquest of Mexico* (Austin, 1956) has treated the shipbuilding activities of López in 1519-1521.

# GLOSSARY

THE FOLLOWING words are defined in terms of the specific uses to which they were put in this study.

*Alcalde mayor*—an administrative and judicial officer over a small area (not unlike a modern county) wherein a number of small towns were subordinate to a larger one

*Alcalde ordinario*—a municipal official whose duties combine administrative and judicial functions; commonly thought of as the approximation of our mayor, though certain duties resemble those of our justice of the peace. Often simply termed alcalde

*Alguacil mayor*—a peace officer with duties approximating those of a sheriff

*Aranzada*—a variable measure for agricultural land, commonly ranging between 10 and 12 acres.

*Arroba*—a measure of weight, approximating 25 pounds

*Audiencia*—a leading agency of colonial government, primarily judicial in its function but also possessed of administrative responsibilities; it contained variable numbers of judges, depending upon the size and significance of the area involved.

*Caballería*—the piece of land given a cavalryman for the services rendered by him during the conquest or early occupation of a region; a variable measure of land which frequently approximated 400-500 acres

*Castellano*—an old Spanish coin, a fiftieth part of a gold mark, of varying value but approximating 490 maravedis (which see); a forerunner of the peso

*Corregidor*—an official resembling the alcalde mayor, with the corregidor considered the more effective representative of royal authority

*Corregimiento*—the area under the jurisdiction of the corregidor; likewise the office of the corregidor

*Encomendero*—the holder or master of an encomienda (which see)

*Encomienda*—the fiduciary interest of a Spaniard in Indian laborers entrusted to him for a specified period under certain conditions

*Factor*—in military operations the official charged with the distribution of supplies to the soldiers; in political life an official charged with collecting the tribute and other revenue due the crown

*Maravedi*—the smallest Spanish monetary unit

*Pesquisa secreta*—a secret inquiry into an official's administration; a secret marshaling of evidence concerning an official which is to be presented to higher authorities

*Quintal*—a measure of weight, approximating 100 pounds or four arrobas

*Real*—a silver coin equivalent to a tomín; one-eighth of a gold peso

*Residencia*—an investigation of an official's administration of his post, conducted at the end of his term of office

*Tomín*—a silver coin equivalent to a real; one-eighth of a gold peso

*Visita*—the inspection, during his tenure, of an official's conduct of his office

*Visitador*—a judge or inspector authorized to conduct a visita

# INDEX